Larry McMurtry's Texas: Evolution of the Myth

*Larry McMurtry, participant, conference on the "Texas Literary Tradition,"
at The University of Texas; at Austin, March 24–26, 1983, part of UT's
Centennial observance.*

— Photo courtesy Larry Murphy

Larry McMurtry's Texas
Evolution of the Myth

Lera Patrick Tyler Lich

EAKIN PRESS ★ Austin, Texas

FIRST EDITION

Copyright © 1987
By Lera Patrick Tyler Lich

Published in the United States of America
By Eakin Press, P.O. Box 23069, Austin, Texas 78735

ISBN 0-89015-613-1

Library of Congress Cataloging-in-Publication Data

Lich, Lera Patrick Tyler, 1948-
    Larry McMurtry's Texas.

    Bibliography: p.
    1. McMurtry, Larry — Knowledge — Texas.   2. McMurtry, Larry — Settings.
3. Texas in literature.   4. Myth in literature.   I. Title.
PS3563.A319Z765   1987   813'.54   87-24314
ISBN 0-89015-613-1

To those patient souls who have taught me

Contents

Acknowledgments

This monograph has been possible only because many people have generously given time, knowledge, and financial support. First, I want to thank the English Department at the University of New Orleans, especially Raeburn Miller, Mary Wagoner, Malcolm Magaw, and John Cooke. Larry McMurtry graciously answered my letters and granted permission to use the Kunkel letters at the University of Houston Library. I also wish to acknowledge the assistance given by the Special Collections staff at the University of Houston Library in working with the McMurtry materials housed there.

I thank Encino Press, Dial Press, the University of New Mexico Press, and Simon and Schuster for permission to quote from Larry McMurtry's works. Ann Graham of the Barker History Library and Donaly E. Brice of the Texas State Archives provided research assistance. I thank Kay Satchell, Mary Ann Mosty-Hamilton-Parker, and Anabel Rivera for their clerical assistance and Monte Lewis for his inside information on Archer City. The Therese Kayser Lindsey Lectures at Southwest Texas State University in 1979 aroused my interest in this project, and Robert W. Walts's publication of that series has been a valuable reference.

To my family, which has been perennially dedicated to learning, goes my heartfelt gratitude. My parents provided inspiration, and their expectations led the way. The generosity of my aunts, Arline Tyler and Paralee Tyler Vowels, enabled me to start this study. Ultimately, though, I thank my husband Glen and our three children James, Stephen, and Elizabeth, for their patience and encouragement helped me to complete this project.

The ruins of Archer City's picture show. The theater closed in the 1950s, and fire later gutted the building.

— Photograph by Glen E. Lich

Larry McMurtry's Texas:
Evolution of the Myth

It was the sky that was Texas, the sky that welcomed me back. The land I didn't care for all that much — it was bleak and monotonous and full of ugly little towns. The sky was what I had been missing, and seeing it again in its morning brightness made me realize suddenly why I hadn't been myself for many months. It had such depth and such spaciousness and such incredible compass, it took so much in and circled one with such a tremendous generous space that it was impossible not to feel more intensely with it above you.

— *All My Friends Are Going to Be Strangers*

Introduction

So we beat on, boats against the current,
borne back ceaselessly into the past.
          — F. Scott Fitzgerald
          The Great Gatsby

Several years ago I visited an old family farm in the sandy red hills of western Georgia. The estate, now preserved as a working museum, has on it buildings and equipment used by prosperous yeoman farmers in the later nineteenth century to maintain their self-sufficiency in a fickle economy. Upon entering the toolshed, a small, musty lean-to on the side of the barn, I was struck by the *smell*. A dozen buried memories flashed before me, twenty-year-old memories of that same smell in my own Georgian-Texan grandfather's toolshed, memories of him and of my childhood experiences with him. The transportation from one world to another was astoundingly rapid and complete. Most of those memories have again been lost by the clutter of more recent experiences, but the lesson remains: our childhood world is with us forever, frustratingly near and distant.

1

The conditions of our upbringings are, of course, not our choice. To children, they don't matter. Instead, we appreciate the immediate; we are fascinated and made curious by what we see and hear and feel and touch. We accept our environment, respond to it, and in one way or another, become products of it.

As we grow into young adults, attitudes change. Those same developing critical and analytical skills which help us understand Socrates or Shakespeare or Keats now teach us to judge our immediate world — often with disdain, for that world may seem simplistic, harsh, restrictive. We put aside our childhood experiences, envying those who could grow up in more stimulating environments and declaring that our children will have better opportunities.

Then, one day, we enter an old toolshed somewhere, and the musty mixture of aged carpentry tools and wood brings back our childhood world and all the fascination that world held. This power of recollection is, to me, one of the distinguishing traits of an artist or poet or writer: *the capacity to recall memories many of us have buried.* And if that is true, then, in the end, it is the local and immediate experience and its context that provide the writer's creative universe. Later experiences improve the capacity to express that world.

Because I am a Texan interested in how writers have dealt with the ambivalent experience of being creative Texans, the world and works of Larry McMurtry hold special interest. As Texans, most of us think that we have a special, and difficult, environment with which to contend. Texas writers have frequently bemoaned their alienation from established eastern publishing houses and critics.[1] And, in truth, our state has produced no writers equal to its great size and significance in the American experience. McMurtry, however, is one of the best novelists from this arid soil. His literary development and his life hold some interesting examples in the writer's use of and release from local experience.

Writers from the West appear to be in an enviable position. Many, like McMurtry, were reared in an environment which fosters the great American epic given credence by Frederick Jackson Turner: on the frontier man stood as individual, touching with outstretched arms the two worlds of civilization and wilderness but standing in neither. This hero, especially if a cowboy, was a true adventurer like Jason, Odysseus, or Beowulf. Historical heroes like Sam Houston and Charlie Goodnight and dozens of Texas Rangers and local cattlemen further reified the tradition.[2] Historical figures and events can, however ironically, distort the truth; facts, legends, and visions tend to blur into local mythology which then becomes part of a collective spirit. Consequently, we Westerners still see our sons as Huck Finns, free from cultural inhibitions and more clever than those well-educated boys in the East. We still see ourselves as stubborn and independent in times of crises. Our literature reflects who we think we are and who we would like to be. Our "toughest" Western fiction has a romantic bias, for in this landscape individualism comes by necessity.

We are all "the product, in fact, the image of a place," commented the late Texas poet and novelist R. G. Vliet.[3] Those writers fortunate or unfortunate enough to be born in Texas must live with two gigantic images: the fantasy world of cowboys, Indians, and rich oilmen and the real world of hardship, subsistence, and stagnation. Perhaps because of this latter, threatening existence, Texas did not produce native writers of national distinction until J. Frank Dobie, Fred Gipson, and Katherine Anne Porter emerged between 1930 and 1960. Before their time, most prose about Texas had come from writers only casually acquainted with the state — from sixteenth-century travel literature, which even then stressed fabulous legends of golden cities, to nineteenth-century dime novels that made every man a hero.

When native writers did begin producing creditable fiction, they were confronted with several problems. William Pilkington, critic of the state's literature, explains that Texas writers too often "fall victim to the very qualities that attracted them in the first place" when they yield "to the temptation to be romantic about the past or lyrical about the landscape." [4] Today most writers continue to be preoccupied with Texas's colorful past, especially its heroic values, and they retain a passion for its harsh and demanding land.

Does the myth of Texas, then, stimulate a writer? Can it act as a creative force on those young people who are born a part of it and later develop into writers? Or does its romanticism and provincialism inhibit serious writing? Traditionally, because Texans like to think they are people of energy and action, they seldom tolerate time for reflection and words. Small-town practices and old-time values greet the writer with tepid hostility.

I turn, then, to Larry McMurtry, perhaps the most widely read and most successful of the present generation of Texas writers, to answer in part those issues. Three of his novels have been made into award-winning films: *Hud, The Last Picture Show,* and *Terms of Endearment.* His works have received national recognition while most other Texas novelists write in obscurity. How has he handled his Texas heritage? The answer lies in a study of the creative forces in McMurtry's life.

Son and grandson of frontier cattlemen, he descends from the Western environment. Furthermore, he grew up in a crucial place at a crucial time when frontier, or post-frontier, values were challenged by the urban world.[5] McMurtry uses those childhood experiences upon which writers depend, but he has not idealized them. Consequently, while he speaks in the native language of setting, a language which generates characters who are functions of their setting, he avoids sentimentality. The worlds he creates are grotesque and powerful and touching. The people cope — as he had to cope — with a compelling but frequently stunting and unpredictable environment. In McMurtry's own life and in his fiction, setting victimizes and twists character.

As one of the leading critics of Texas society and Texas fiction, McMurtry also confronts the new dimension in the Texas myth, the conflict between land-based values and the urban world. At a time when some writers are shoring up land values with more mythology, McMurtry has his own way of acknowledging the conflict.

The issues raised here are of more than local concern in the end, for the issue of what makes and destroys imagination is important to anyone concerned with creation. The magical product of past and present, physical and imagined worlds, reveals many layers of thought which can be uncovered in part by careful analysis of a writer's world. This brief literary biography will discuss the effects of environment on a writer and his characters. McMurtry's development as a novelist has passed through several stages which are the basis of this study's five chapters. The places he has lived and the places he has created — his actual and fictional homes — blend into settings which he has both denied and accepted. The first two chapters discuss Archer County, McMurtry's childhood home, and its fictional counterpart Thalia, setting for his first novels. The third chapter deals with McMurtry's next home, Houston, and the fourth with his departure from Texas and attempt to find new settings. The final chapter explains his return to Texas and his choice of a home in the mythic past of the Western frontier. I chose this approach because McMurtry's tightly woven relationship of setting and character becomes central to understanding his writing. Regional values addressed in his novels penetrate regionalism, becoming a fictional ethology. And dilemmas faced by both Mc-Murtry and his characters are common to many people, not just Texans.

Furthermore, the Texas myth transcends itself because, in a way, it is a rambunctious brother to the American myth — the promise of a land of independence, adventure, and profit. Mc-Murtry suggests that "on the rims of the West — and perhaps, in America, only there — one can still know for a moment the frontier emotion, . . . the sense of an openness so vast it still challenges." [6] Here perhaps a Gatsbian dream still exists; here is an analogy to that "enchanted moment" when man "held his breath in the presence of this continent . . . face to face for the last time in history with something commensurate with his capacity for wonder." [7]

1   The Home Setting

Settings of any kind are most dramatic when first viewed from the edges. Archer County, Texas, is situated twenty miles south of the Oklahoma border and just west of the ninety-eighth meridian, the "institutional fault line" that, according to Walter Prescott Webb, separates two civilizations of the United States. Hostile Indians, inclement weather, and dearth of natural resources west of this boundary stalled migration of Americans and Europeans for decades. Finally, in the 1880s, elimination of raiding Indian tribes and invention of the windmill enabled settlers to push onward. When the desperate and restless moved onto the flat and treeless expanses of mid-America, Webb asserts "practically every institution that was carried across it was either broken and remade or else greatly altered." [1]

Attitudes about society, religion, law, and family changed. Farmers, the social and economic backbone of rural Eastern America, here found themselves inferior, laboring like beasts to scratch from the earth what it would provide. Their cattlemen-neighbors, on the other hand, ranged over the plains from atop horses, looking far into the expanses and feeling a sense of conquest. Even then, cattlemen and cowboys were heroes of the West. They formed a masculine society in the vastness of frontier freedom. Laws were construed according to immediate needs, each man his own god and the law-giver on his own land.

Nowhere is this heroic frontier setting more obvious than at its threshold along the ninety-eighth meridian. Along an ocean shore the powerful pull and mystery of the sea on one side and of the land on the other creates tension and inspiration. Larry McMurtry's boyhood world at the edge of the plains environment contains similar threat and strength. In the 1880s his grandparents, William Jefferson McMurtry and Louisa Frances McMurtry, moved to Archer County after a brief residency in Denton County, Texas. Originally from Benton County, Missouri, they were among the thousands of Scotch-Irish families migrating from the Upper South to frontier fringes.[2] They bought a half-section of Archer County land, located along an old military road then used as a cattle trail. There the nine McMurtry sons, from their barn-top vantage on Idiot Ridge, glimpsed the last of the great cattle drives passing over the country. They saw heroic figures on horseback moving out and poor farmers moving in.[3] One by one, the sons of William J. McMurtry chose cowboy life, not on cattle trails — for by the turn of the century the long drives were over — but on enormous ranches near Clarendon in the Texas Panhandle. Jim McMurtry earned his first money breaking horses for a dollar a head; his later years were spent wealthy and crippled. Disease, accidents, and numerous other misfortunes beset indomitable Johnny McMurtry; the endless vicissitudes of his life are the makings of a saga.

Recollections of these men who idolized "the god whose principal myth was the myth of the Cowboy, the ground of whose divinity was the Range" and whose livelihood was "filled with rituals of that faith"[4] frame Larry McMurtry's *In A Narrow Grave,* a collection of essays published in 1968. McMurtry sees this cowboy-god "as Old Man Goodnight, or as Teddy Blue, or as my Uncle Johnny . . . but the one thing that is sure is that he was a horseman, and a god of the country. His home was the frontier, and his mythos celebrates those masculine ideals appropriate to a frontier."[5]

William Jefferson McMurtry and his wife lived near their boys in the Panhandle for about six years but returned in 1925 to Archer County with son William Jefferson, Jr., who would be Larry McMurtry's father. By then most of Texas was slowly moving into a post-frontier society, but progress was especially stunted in areas like Archer County, where old Texas traditions lingered. Furthermore, the land was harsh and the agricultural economy depressed. Innovations were accepted reluctantly, and people generally stayed put. Frontier ways were retained and adapted in the memories of the old ones. They and their children sometimes maintained an isolated life, retelling the frontier days, or sometimes moved into nearby towns, establishing a new communal spirit.

The post-frontier society that emerged thus entailed two distinct ways of life. The rancher who lived out of town retained a frontier ethos. He owned his land both literally and spiritually and received from it his identity. Ranch life was male-oriented and demanded independence and initiative. The rancher was stereotypically an eccentric man who avoided most social institutions and recognized the world as vast and harsh. As rural towns like Archer City grew modestly, often populated by old ranching families persuaded into town life by wives or children, nineteenth-century values from the East were established and the institutional fault line blurred. The matrons of the town developed and preserved what they envisioned as the good, wholesome life. Young people were instilled with the religion and morals to continue their town's rectitude. Order and communal attitudes were established — at the price of initiative and independence. On some common grounds, however, the ranchers of the plains and the citizens of the small town met: they shared a fear that urbanization and modernization could and would reach out and destroy a way of life.

As oil fields were discovered across the state, sleepy Texas awoke with oil fever. When worker families moved in and out of towns, old-timers reinforced their values to prevent social upheaval. Change occurred anyway. Some of the old settlers were fortunate enough to find themselves wealthy with little effort while others lost the land that had been their identity or sulked at evil industry. Those towns untouched by the discovery of oil did not escape the twentieth century long. World War II drew away young men, who either by fate or choice never returned. Closed rural society was pried open and began to falter. Children of prosperous old-timers went off to school — and stayed away. The opportunities of urban life tempted other energetic people to cities. Consequently, adults who chose to remain in rural Texas held tight to their beliefs and morals while the young increasingly saw the future on the other side of the city limits sign.

The era was fertile boyhood ground for a future novelist. Growing up in a transition of time and place, Larry McMurtry witnessed with some personal detachment the passing of one culture and the rise of another. The experience is common to regional writers: it has been the background of many Southern novelists. "Only at a crisis point in history, when one definite form of society is disappearing and another is emerging," comments Richard Gray in his study of modern Southern fiction, "can writers as a group employ their inheritance as a 'source of ideas' and metaphors and still be sufficiently detached from their inheritance to be critical of it." [6] McMurtry was the first Western writer, however, to use such a crisis as had been a creative impetus in the South for sixty years.

Larry McMurtry was born in Wichita Falls, the city nearest Archer County, on June 3, 1936. His parents, William Jefferson and Hazel Ruth McMurtry, lived with his grandparents on a ranch eighteen miles from town. Neither the McMurtrys of Archer County nor relatives in the Panhandle had reconciled the death of Old Texas. At family reunions near Clarendon, the old days were relived, the myth recreated. In a 1978 address at Southwest Texas State University in San Marcos, McMurtry discussed his background:

> I grew up just at the time when rural and soil traditions in Texas were really, for the first time, being seriously challenged by urban tradition. . . . Right here on the one hand were old men, grandparents, who had come in and settled the country and who had a deep belief and commitment to 19th century virtues, fundamentalist virtues, to the agrarian and rural way of life, to the traditions of the soil; and before they knew it, their grandchildren, if not their children, had gone off to the city: . . . and before the frontier generation could totally die, an urban generation had come into being whose ways and customs and manners were often in conflict with theirs.[7]

Those old men had as boys gazed into the passing of the West from the tops of the Idiot Ridge barns. By the 1940s they were cynical cattlemen who saw "the ideals of the faith degenerate, the rituals fall from use, the principal myth become corrupt." The land had been left "to strange and godless heirs." [8]

The new generation could never replace the old one. This assumption becomes the thematic core of Larry McMurtry's early novels. As a youth, however, associations with old-timers often produced discomfort. "With most of my uncles I had no rapport at all," says McMurtry. "To their practiced eye it must have been evident from the first that I was not going to turn out to be a cattleman." The uncles apparently would have appreciated a Huck Finn more than a Larry McMurtry. "For one thing, I wasn't particularly mean, and in the West the mischief quotient is still a popular standard for measuring the appearance of approvable masculine qualities in a youngster. . . . Mean kids meant strength in time of need, and how could the elders be sure that a bookish and suspiciously observant youngster like myself might not in time disgrace the line?" Indeed, the relatives' indifference impressed McMurtry profoundly. "I knew from an early age that I could never meet their standard," he admitted, "and since in those days theirs was the only standard I knew existed I was the more defensive around them. Indeed scared." [9]

The ambivalence of McMurtry's attitude toward Texas begins here in an admixture of attraction and scorn for the cowboy uncles who were his archetypes for both heroic and villainous characters. Despite the dramatic aura of their lives, the values manifested in these uncles were not "wholly admirable" to young McMurtry.[10] While he grew older and listened year after year to their tales of fearless and free cowboy days, he realized the inconsistency of the McMurtry situation. Family members gathered at reunions in part to revitalize the myth. These mythmakers had, however, sold out to another world — maybe unwillingly or maybe unknowingly. The placid country-club setting of the reunions emphasized that point. About the same time in his life, McMurtry discovered another world, the world of *Don Quixote* in particular and of books in general:

> . . . I am lucky to have found so satisfying a replacement as *Don Quixote* offered. And yet, that first life has not quite died in me — not quite. I missed it only by the width of a generation and, as I was growing up, heard the whistle of its departure. Not long after I entered the pastures of the empty page I realized that the place where all my stories start is the heart faced suddenly with the loss of its country, its customary and legendary range.[11]

Ironically, the boy regarded with indifference by these old-timers eventually became the McMurtry whose name is most often associated with the Texas myth.

Moving into Archer City hardly offered a more broadening experience for the boy. While he had acquired from ranch life an ambivalent respect for cowboys and their world, he acquired less than that for his hometown. After living in and around Archer City for eighteen years, he learned that small towns stagnated. The vision of most adults there extended not to the frontiersman's horizon but just to the boundaries of the community.

Two separate societies, male and female, operated in rural towns like Archer City. Cut off from frontier experience, men sought new sources of masculine identity while retaining the traditional Western discomfort with female society. Sexual segregation was further enforced by the women, few of whom ventured beyond traditional roles. Because the small-town atmosphere encouraged women to perpetuate these roles, they lived in the community with more assurance and with determination not to disrupt the sexual and social barriers. Consequently, McMurtry asserts that normal male-female interaction, even in the privacy of the home, was not observable. "Though it seems incredible," he comments, "we probably derived a more realistic view of women from the movies than we got from our homelife and our social experience." [12]

An intelligent person was an additional discomfort to those not confident of their roles and less endowed with sensitivity. "Bookish" individuals, like young McMurtry, were often ostracized. McMurtry recalls several youths who were thrust into toilets because they exhibited their intelligence. One old man in Archer City spent his days and nights reading and filled his backyard junkpile with book catalogs. No one communicated with him. He was, McMurtry guesses, the town intellectual. His counterparts and successors are all in the city, along with "the brainy, the imaginative, the beautiful, even the energetic. None of them can find much reason for staying in the towns." [13]

As the town's vitality disappeared, the activities of its young became an increasingly crucial source of identity. Townspeople bragged of football teams and homecoming queens, and, in fact, lived vicariously in these high school celebrities who seemed to have extraordinary sex appeal. A boy was successful if he graduated with a long list of extracurricular achievements; the men courted him if he was a football star and the women adored him if he was a church youth-group leader. McMurtry notes that "most of my small-town contemporaries spent their high school years trying desperately to be good athletes, because the attitude of adults had them quite convinced that their sexual identity depended upon their athletic performance." After their high school experience these youths faced the difficulty of finding a new identity. Some realized the narrowness of the town's view and eventually abandoned it, "but others of them have not shed it yet, and never will." [14]

In 1954 McMurtry graduated from Archer City High School. Once out of school, he was one who easily shed himself of hometown convictions if, indeed, he ever truly believed in them. Since 1954 his feelings for Archer City have ranged from hostile to indifferent to generous, but he has never, since the age of twelve, preferred the rural scene to the world of fiction. "I came away from it far from convinced that the country is a good place to form character, acquire fullness, or lead the Good Life." With typical McMurtry iconoclasm, he refutes Texas Romanticism: "Sentimentalists are still fond of saying that nature is the best teacher — I have known many Texans who felt that way, and most of them live and die in woeful ignorance." [15]

McMurtry attended Rice University in Houston for one semester in fall 1954. Rejecting its math and science orientation, he returned to his home region and enrolled as an English major at North Texas State College in Denton.

While at North Texas, McMurtry read avidly. Faulkner was among his favorite American writers. He studied a number of the works of the Beat Generation of the 1950s and wrote two pieces of literary criticism about the movement, one in 1957 for *Avesta,* the college literary magazine, and another in 1960 for *Janus,* the Rice University literary magazine.[16] Jack Kerouac's *On the Road* (1957) in particular stimulated young McMurtry, and its influences show up especially in his urban novels. Despite an interest in contemporary fiction, McMurtry claims that his readings of nineteenth-century, non-American writers — Eliot, Hardy, Dickens, Tolstoy, Balzac, and Stendhal — made the most permanent impression on his career.[17]

During his last two years as an undergraduate, McMurtry experimented in writing poetry, short stories, and essays. Most of the short stories were, according to McMurtry, unsuccessful fiction. Toward the end of his undergraduate studies, however, he began to draw upon his frontier heritage, and this writing was productive and satisfying personally. In the 1957–58 term McMurtry and two other seniors edited a short-lived underground publication, *Coexistence Review*. In its first issue appeared "Granddad's End," an early version of the climactic passage of *Horseman, Pass By*.[18]

Although this short piece varies considerably from the final work, it is critically important for McMurtry's beginnings as a novelist. When questioned about his writing process, McMurtry affirmed that all of his novels start with a culminating scene. "I can tell that the scene ends something. . . . I don't know what's ended, and the writing of the novel is a process in which I discover how these people get themselves to this scene." [19] McMurtry found the idea for his first novel in "Granddad's End," and immediately after graduation from North Texas in June 1958, he started the work. By autumn of that year, he had a completed manuscript and was beginning graduate studies in English at Rice. Almost three years later, after receiving a master's degree from Rice and while studying as a Wallace Stegner Fellow at Stanford University, McMurtry saw at the age of twenty-four the publication of his first novel.

McMurtry's collegiate years at North Texas and Rice may have broadened his perspective on life and they no doubt formed the basis for his urban novels, but they served mainly as years through which to filter his childhood experiences and the themes that emerged from them. In McMurtry's early fiction, traditional rites of passage in a character's life are secondary to the rites of passage of the landscape. The land and its people, on the edge of two worlds, experienced the ebb and flow of civilization and wilderness. By the time of McMurtry's childhood, the struggle, which began as an effort to survive on the frontier and continued as an effort to retain frontier spirit, was inevitably concluding. A keen observer and skillful writer like McMurtry, standing near the point of conflict, uses that drama to create potent fiction. He was born of a people who had lived for years on the fringes of civilization, who could see both into the vastness of the plains and into the culture of the East — into two divergent worlds. He was born in time to see the old frontier tradition pass on to a rural, small-town society and to see that society losing out to a more energetic urban one.

McMurtry uses these experiences to form both Western and modern ethologies. Characters who are a function of their setting and who are trying to survive are placed into compelling but unpredictable and changing environments. From McMurtry's blending of these remembered and imagined worlds comes fiction of unusual strength, poignancy, and realism. His eleven novels published between 1962 and 1987 attest to the potency of both personal experience and the Texas myth.

2   Thalia: The First Literary Home

In the prologue of *Horseman, Pass By,* Lonnie Bannon, the seventeen-year-old narrator, climbs his grandfather's windmill at night, sits on its platform, and gazes out into the flat darkness around him. From there he senses evidence of the new life on the prairie: oil derricks pumping, lights from the town of Thalia blinking, heavy truck motors grinding, and airport beacons from Wichita Falls flashing. This image appropriately begins Larry McMurtry's fiction. Lonnie's feelings under the dark windmill blades re-create emotions felt by those restless McMurtrys of the 1890s who climbed to the tops of barns and stared across the same ridge at passing cattle drives. Lonnie senses the imminence of the future; the McMurtry boys had longed for the glory of the past. The grating conflict between his future and their past, between young and old, reverberates through this small novel, producing a tone often absent in traditional Western fiction.

Horseman, Pass By was first conceived as two short stories, one about a hoof-and-mouth epidemic and another about the death of an old cattleman, while McMurtry was at North Texas State College. His natural curiosity as an enthusiastic literature student to

15

experiment with writing and his youthful sense of loss at the passing of the frontier first combined successfully in this narrative. Although the novel was written in the summer and fall of 1958, the story was revised four or five times before publication in 1961.

Horseman, Pass By narrates events leading up to the death of Homer Bannon, an eighty-four-year-old rancher whose cattle are exterminated because they carry highly contagious hoof-and-mouth disease. Homer's subsequent mental and physical breakdown is set against the brutal vitality of his stepson Hud. In the end, the senile old man is shot, like his cattle, to prevent further suffering. The setting is McMurtry's own country: Archer City becomes McMurtry's mythical Thalia,[1] but the landscape is unaltered.

The elements and people of *Horseman, Pass By* are a microcosm of the modern West. Thus, Homer's ranch — McMurtry's natural symbol of the Old West — has both literal and submerged metaphorical functions. Its decline depicts the end of a particular place and of a fabulous myth.

Traditional Western novels exploit that myth with sentimentality, stock characters, and trite plot. The conventional Western, according to critic John Milton, uses landscape only as an accidental stage to reenact established themes and characters. A "serious" novel, however, is concerned with traditions and physical aspects and with the ways the region affects those living in it.[2] Disease, or fate, may be the natural enemy of Homer Bannon, but a new and more ominous threat will scavenge the remnants of his life. Hud, the mean-spirited mutant of his time and place, brings brutal disaster. Modern rural Texas has spawned grotesques in men like Hud. This environment produces people who, whether rooted in place by inclination or adaptability, are unable to adjust to the changes that setting is undergoing.[3] McMurtry's concern with this maladjustment of modern and Western environments gives the novel its unconventional focus. The predicament of the Bannon family represents the situation of an entire region, and this realism balances the pathos of loss. Critic William Pilkington views Mc-Murtry's study of the Bannon family as "a vivid allegory of the fate of frontier values in the twentieth century."[4] *Horseman, Pass By* is, moreover, the story of the problems of the human condition when shifting landscapes victimize their inhabitants.

All characters in this novel are native to the setting which has

treated them with alternating indifference and cruelty. Survivors
on the land are tough, but even they cannot win against fate.
Homer Bannon, epitome of the cattleman, heroically fights for traditional values. His cattle may be destroyed, but the land sacred to
him will not be violated by modernization, even when it is barren
and useless as a ranch. "Something about this sickness, maybe I
can't do much about, but the oil-field stuff I can. I don't like it an'
I don't aim to have it," he protests. "I guess I'm a queer, contrary
old bastard, but there'll be no holes punched in this land while I'm
here." [5] He knows he cannot defeat the disease, but he tries to protect his heritage and independence. He has few friends and closes
himself off from the small-town ways and religion of his wife. Apparently he is narrow-minded and cantankerous. Through the eyes
of his grandson Lonnie, however, Homer becomes an introspective
and considerate hero, embodying nineteenth-century ideals of industry, independence, and honor. "There wasn't hardly anybody
cared much for Granddad," Lonnie notes after Homer's funeral.
"Some liked him and some were scared of him and a good many
hated his guts. Me and a few cowmen and a few hands and an old-
timer or two loved and respected him some" (135).*

Homer was a man like Teddy Blue or Old Man Goodnight,
the embodiment of qualities young McMurtry saw as honorable.
Hud, who has no lands to tame, horses to break, or herds to drive,
exemplifies traits "not wholly admirable" which a more sophisticated world has produced. He races around in his Cadillac, with
women and whiskey as his companions. To Hud, Homer was a senile old fool.

Conflict between Homer and Hud is the thematic problem of
the novel. Homer's mistakes are from Hud's point of view both
foolish and fatal: Homer blindly married Hud's mother, allowed
Hud's military induction, and bought diseased Mexican cattle. The
younger man's hostility builds as he watches Homer lose strength
and control. "You were Wild Horse Homer Bannon in them days,
an' anything you did was right," Hud admits. "I even thought you
was right myself, the most of the time. Why, I used to think you
was a regular god. I don't no more" (66). The showdown between
Hud and Homer dramatizes the struggle between old and new.

---

* Excerpts from the work being discussed will cite in parentheses page num-
bers of that work.

Like the values he represents, Homer is defeated first by his own misjudgments and finally by the next generation.

Horseman, Pass By is a youthful novel. Within its content and tone is a young writer's mixture of idealism and realism. The tragedy of Homer Bannon is seen through the eyes of an adolescent, a narrator who shares with his author the experiences of a particular time and place. Both narrator and author witness upheaval of tradition, yet neither causes or acts in its drama. Lonnie is, not surprisingly for his age, quite passive, almost a blank. In this early work, McMurtry's strength reposes in his understanding of the land, not in characterization. But that deficiency is outweighed by the reality of the novel, which, according to Pilkington, comes from McMurtry's "leisurely style, his confident and authoritative air, his calm acceptance of an imperfect social environment." He is a novelist "who thoroughly knows himself and his blood's country." [6] John Howard Griffin wrote to McMurtry's agent at Harper and Row that "this is probably the starkest, most truthful, most terrible, and yet beautiful treatment of [the ranching country] I've seen." [7]

Though underdeveloped, Lonnie's character does depict the general frustrations McMurtry's West Texas contemporaries felt. He is restless, like most adolescents. Rural youths, isolated from a brighter and more exciting urban world, are perhaps even more wistful in their yearnings than their urban peers. Lonnie wants "to be off somewhere, with a crowd of laughers and courters and beer drinkers, to go somewhere past Thalia and Wichita and the oil towns and Sno-Cone stands." He wants to go someplace he has never seen. Lonnie realizes that both he and his environment are changing and that he will be unable to live in the world of the past much longer. He laments that "Granddad didn't talk to me much any more, and anyway, Granddad and I were in such separate times and separate places. I had got where I would rather go to Thalia and goof around the square than listen to his old-timy stories" (21). Thalia, however, is "just an empty courthouse square to drive around" (20), and having the black cook and housekeeper Halmea around the ranch only increases his yearnings and his alienation: makes him feel "alone and restless and left out." She and the hands unintentionally have a way of letting "people younger than them know they aren't in the same club" (16–17). Lonnie wants exciting experiences but is restrained, partly because no one around him seems to have reached goals or enjoyed adventures. "All of them," he says of the boys in the area, "wanted more and seemed to end up with less" (117). Even when Homer's hired hand Jesse reminisces to Lonnie about his carefree young years across Western America and tells the youngster "to get out and do your own rarin' and tearin', without no pattern a mine," the advice is melancholic. Being young "sure wears out in a hurry. Or did for me" (19–20).

Additional stress comes to the ranch once the cattle disease is detected, and that tension leaves Lonnie even more alone. One evening, while sitting with Granddad and Grandma, he has "the terrible feeling that things were all out of kilter, all jumbled up." Nonetheless, he "couldn't seem to leave them, the two old ones" (71). Frustrated, Lonnie maliciously shoots frogs and jackrabbits and turtles. He wants to prove himself to, as McMurtry said about his own heritage, "the only standard I knew existed." [8] Because Lonnie wants to be a man for Granddad's cowboys, he struggles to open the hard pasture gate and continues to work in the cattle pens after being injured, but the efforts are futile. After his grandfather's death, Lonnie had no "satisfying replacement" for the lost ranch and the lost world it represents.

Horseman, Pass By contains little explicit autobiographical matter other than the setting but, as an expression of McMurtry's feelings of loss and loneliness, the novel is his catharsis. Nevertheless, *Horseman, Pass By* did not relieve the myth from his soul. In fact, after the release of this book and the movie based on it, his name became increasingly associated with the myth, and privately he was still haunted by the mythic vision. The land and its past still gripped him. During the filming of *Hud,* McMurtry felt the presence of the old ones on the prairies of North Texas. "Looking at the weathered ranch buildings or out across the grassy, shadow-flecked plains, it was easier to believe in the ghost of Old Man Goodnight than in the costume-department darling in huaraches and yellow silk shirt who crossed and recrossed one's path." [9]

In the end, though, Old Man Goodnight and Granddad and the Old West remain unexorcised ghosts to McMurtry. In his fiction they appear as legends and dreams. In one poignant passage from *Horseman, Pass By,* Lonnie glimpses an idyllic Texas — but only in a dream. He and his grandfather were riding across the high country and below them was Texas,

green and brown and graying in the sun, spread wide under the
clear spread of sky like the opening scene in a big Western movie.
There were rolling hills in the north, and cattle grazing here and
there, and strings of horses under the shade trees. Then above us
the little gray clouds began to slip away toward the north like
coyotes in the pastures. We could see creeks winding across the
flats, dark green oak trees growing along their banks. The green
waving acres of mesquite spread out and away from us to the
south and east. I saw the highways cutting through the bright un-
shaded towns, and I kept expecting Granddad to say something
to me. But he was relaxed, looking across the land. Finally he
swung his feet into the stirrups and we rode down together into
the valley toward some ranch I couldn't see, the Llano Estacado
or the Old Matador. (60)

Although McMurtry admits that "some element of emotional
autobiography" exists in almost all novels, he considers his works
to be autobiographical primarily in their description of Archer
County. "The books are about a place, a very particular region,
and the place goes a long way toward determining the books'
tone." He continues by explaining that "while the books are partly
about me, partly about a place, partly about our time, they are, I
hope, chiefly about the characters who live them." [10] He writes of a
world and of a people losing in a land of changing landscapes and
mindscapes.

After the publication of *Horseman, Pass By,* McMurtry taught
intermittently, first at Texas Christian University in Fort Worth
(1961–1962) and later at Rice. Harper and Row had meanwhile
accepted his second manuscript, written while he was a graduate
student at Rice, and in 1963, *Leaving Cheyenne,* the second of the
Thalia trilogy and one of the most critically acclaimed of his novels,
was published. By that time McMurtry was again in Houston, this
time as an instructor of creative writing at Rice. As one of Texas's
foremost young writers, he wrote essays and reviews. While his critical attitude developed, his fiction moved off the homeplace, and in
that strain late in 1965 he wrote a third novel, the last set in Thalia.

McMurtry's biographer Charles D. Peavy claims that this
novel resulted from a bitter three-day visit to Archer City in 1965
and was written in six weeks while McMurtry was still piqued at
the town.[11] McMurtry himself states that the title *The Last Picture
Show* was originally conceived as a collection of short stories, simi-

lar in tone to the novel and intended "to dramatize the effects of the gradual seepage of people out of the small town." [12]

While the earlier books used Western setting and Western myth, *The Last Picture Show* debunks the nostalgic image of small-town life. *Horseman, Pass By* and *Leaving Cheyenne* had been written to release McMurtry from ghosts of the frontier tradition, and *The Last Picture Show* was written at least in part to expel the hostility he felt for Archer City. Even though the stimulus for writing this novel may have been a recent visit to his hometown, an antipathy toward Archer City had existed for years. His experiences there as a youth and in urban San Francisco and Houston as an adult produced a bitter realism about small-town citizens and their values. The fictional consequence of McMurtry's animosity is a satire on religion, manners, education, and sex in small-town Texas.

Other Texas writers frequently remember their childhood homes fondly. In small towns a person could touch the past, according to writer John Graves, and "like all human pasts — and all human presents and all human futures — it had vast imperfections," but people were "glad to touch it." [13] A similar nostalgia is evident in McMurtry's attitude about the ranching country, but Archer City is treated with cynicism. The ranch and its traditions were, of course, part of his personal identity, but in the town he was isolated and treated indifferently by people who were, in his judgment, misguided. As creator of Thalia, McMurtry invents an especially revealing image in a satirical passage from *The Last Picture Show*:

> It was one of those days when it seemed to Christian people that the Lord must have lost all patience with the town. It was a wonder he hadn't simply destroyed it by fire, like he had Sodom, and since the heat at midafternoon that day was 109 degrees He could easily have done so simply by making the sun a little hotter. [14]

McMurtry almost destroys the town — but not quite. Time will do that for him.

Thalia sits in barren landscape. The appearance of the town and its surrounding countryside is "flat and empty," a place to go insane, a place to be lonely. A vast expanse around the town and a wind that blows into it seem to choke out life. As the novel opens, a north wind whips through the street and Billy, a mentally retarded orphan, pointlessly sweeps at the dust. Like the first image in

Horseman, Pass By, this scene is a particularly appropriate start: the town, like Billy, is unconscious of its perversion and foolishly believes itself to be doing good for decent folk.

Like *Horseman, Pass By,* this novel narrates rites of passage of both place and character. Sonny Crawford, the central character of *The Last Picture Show,* is a high school senior, a member of the football team which, like the town, is a loser. Because his mother is dead and his father is a drug addict, Sonny supports himself and proudly exhibits that spark of independence typical of Western heroes. Furthermore, the good people of the town like him, so in the absence of parents, he receives paternal guidance from Sam the Lion and maternal guidance from a curious variety of older women. Although his character is only partially developed, McMurtry creates for him a likeable ethos through the reactions of the townspeople and through his lonely life. As the year progresses, Sonny realizes that the town is dying, a situation made evident by Sam's death and the closing of the picture show. As the town wanes, Sonny matures from a typical local boy to a young man emotionally alienated from crowd and town.

Sam the Lion represents McMurtry's old ones, and as such is the moral guide of *The Last Picture Show,* but he is aged and crippled. Sam was once a rancher and an oilman and later a car dealer. At the time of the novel he simply "took care of things, particularly of boys" (4) and owns the town's main places of interest: the cafe, picture show, and pool hall. He has tragically lost three sons and his vitality, but he remains faithful to principles. He does not tolerate boys mistreating Billy, will not let Lois Farrow leave her husband, and, in the end, leaves a will that confounds the town by its puzzling generosity.

Three older women in the town also defy its conformity. Genevieve, the late-night waitress in the cafe, is an archetypal earth mother. Sonny is strongly attracted to her and seeks out her advice and companionship on many lonely nights. Lois Farrow appears to be the town's free spirit, but she feels the hold of the land and knows, perhaps more strongly than anyone else, the madness it brings. Unafraid of gossip and careless of the town's attitude toward her, Lois escapes from insanity through money, men, and alcohol. Yet, despite scandalous behavior, she is no hypocrite. She sympathizes with pitiful Joe Bob Blanton when his minister-father and Thalia reject him. Understanding that the father's expectations caused the boy's immoral behavior, she openly sides with the youth. Lois is also the woman who truly initiates Sonny into manhood, for his affair with his coach's wife Ruth Popper only prepared him for the final rite of passage with Lois. She advises the impressionable and confused young Sonny to have more assurance: "It's not how much you're worth to the woman. It's how much you're worth to yourself. It's what you really can feel that makes you nice." Lois admits that she is "rich and mean" to most men because "that's what they want and deserve," but she thinks Sonny different and worth training (254–255). Ruth Popper is the most pathetic of the women. Worn-out but pretty, this middle-aged wife of the town's foul-tempered, misogynistic high school coach seeks Sonny's affections because of sexual and maternal longings. A foil to Lois Farrow, she is pale, stiff-moving, fearful, and cautious. Her life becomes tolerable through fantasies about Sonny and afternoons with him.

The affair with Ruth Popper evokes some pathos in a novel otherwise filled with satire. In the life of Thalia's young people, McMurtry finds the primary targets for attack. Charlene Duggs, Sonny's steady girlfriend early in the novel, demonstrates what the town can produce. Unimaginative and ignorant, her passions are movie stars and toilet water. She saves partially used gum on the bottom of the picture show chair and pops it back in her mouth after a few gulping kisses with Sonny. Jacy Farrow, Lois's spoiled daughter, is Charlene's opposite. She is attractive and egocentric. Kissing on the school bus "made her feel a little like a movie star: she could bring beauty and passion into the poor kids' lives" (75). She joins the "fastest crowd" from Wichita because "for a rich, pretty girl like herself the most immoral thing imaginable would be to belong to a slow crowd" (83).

Most of the boys of Thalia receive their standards for masculine identity not from men like Sam the Lion but from a football coach who is lazy, fat, and latently homosexual. Coach Popper, in fact, invents the false accusation that John Cecil, the high school's English teacher, is a homosexual. Ironically, the innocent is fired and the guilty continues in his position. Not surprisingly, the sexual activities of the high school boys are misdirected: they copulate with a blind heifer and solicit intercourse between innocent Billy and the town's car-hop prostitute. Joe Bob, the preacher's son, picks up and modestly molests a five-year-old girl to avoid preaching a revival sermon. Here, too, McMurtry points an ironic finger at the hypocrites of the older generation. Joe Bob's father, with typical Thalia martyrdom, uses the incident of his son's "depravity" to preach a "triumphant" sermon of "self-sacrifice" as the adolescent sits in jail playing checkers with Lois Farrow.

The Last Picture Show has its version of Hud. Abilene, the pool shark and roughneck, is reckless and self-assured. While old men like Sam make mistakes, albeit knowingly, like betting on the local football team, Abilene is realistic — and he wins. He treats women, including Lois Farrow, indifferently, plays with them with the same cold pleasure that he exhibits during a pool game.

Of Thalia's adolescents, only Sonny shows any signs of maturing as the novel progresses. The affair with Mrs. Popper makes him different emotionally, so he no longer feels like participating in boyish activities or in sports. The death of Sam the Lion, graduation from high school, and his foolish elopement with Jacy Farrow further isolate him from Thalia. He is one of the many mixed-up kids McMurtry knew in Archer City, and with his development McMurtry shows increasing confidence in himself. *Horseman, Pass By* hesitantly reveals the emotions of Lonnie, but in Sonny the author develops a more complete picture of a confused young man.

As the novel reaches its conclusion, Sonny is profoundly lonely and depressed. "He had just begun to realize how hard it was to get from day to day if one felt hopeless" (261). Each day was "another one of those mornings when no one was there" (271). Standing on the sidelines of the football game the next fall, "he felt like he wasn't even *in* town — he felt he wasn't anywhere" (260). Sonny cannot, however, leave Thalia. Something, maybe fear or maybe memories, holds him there. In despair, one day he tries but stops at the city limits sign and looks beyond the town where the world is excruciatingly empty. "As empty as he felt and as empty as the country looked it was too risky going out into it — he might be blown around for days like a broomweed in the wind" (277). When Sonny turns around, though, and stops to view the town, it "looked raw, scraped by the wind, as empty as the country. It didn't look like the town it had been when he was in high school, in the days of Sam the Lion" (277).

Both the town and Sonny pass into another age as the story of *The Last Picture Show* is narrated. The message of its passing is the essence that extends beyond any immediate bitterness which generated the novel. Towns like Thalia and Archer City die; their vitality and moral responsibility are depleted, and life seeps away.

Perhaps McMurtry shared with Sonny a sense of guilt at the conclusion of *The Last Picture Show*. Had he exploited Archer City as Sonny had Ruth Popper? Fascination and some tenderness held Sonny to her for a while, but she was easily forgotten when a more attractive female became available. Yet, in the final page, Sonny returns to Ruth. He might resume the affair, but it will be tenuous. Sonny is too lonely and isolated to be truly happy with anyone now. McMurtry is also too alienated to be content with Archer City. More attractive places have naturally drawn him away — but he returns to the town from time to time, and the antipathy he felt waned. In 1971, seven years after finishing *The Last Picture Show*, McMurtry wrote a review of the movie version, in which he admitted that "Archer City had not been cruel to me, only honestly indifferent, and my handling of many characters in the book represented a failure of generosity for which I blame no one but myself." [15]

The ironic dedication of *The Last Picture Show* to McMurtry's hometown masks mixed feelings. The final essay of *In A Narrow Grave*, written about two years after *The Last Picture Show*, also reveals ambivalence: "I am critical of the past, yet apparently attracted to it"; McMurtry admits, "and though I am even more critical of the present I am also quite clearly attracted to *it*." [16] The town had not given him the intellectual stimulus he needed, but it unknowingly provided valuable prototypes and themes.

McMurtry's Thalia speaks for many small towns after World War II. Like the Bannon ranch, this town's decline marks the end of a particular place and of traditions attached to that place. The last of the Thalia trilogy likewise marks the end of one phase of McMurtry's writing. Since *The Last Picture Show* is only peripherally related to the Western myth, with its publication McMurtry shed some of his image as Western writer. Gaining self-confidence and trying new approaches, he expelled himself from the Western myth; however, expulsion from the garden is part of the myth too. Another part of the story is the struggle to return someday, at least for a while. Despite McMurtry's many valedictions, that desire remains.

As McMurtry matured as a writer, his attachment to rural Texas seemed to vanish. More interesting subjects appeared and his focus shifted. Thus, *The Last Picture Show* ended, for twenty years, Larry McMurtry's use of rural settings and pointed him toward the next phase of his writing: the misadventures of young adults who choose sophisticated urban life and their misfortunes in a society that has few traditions or standards.

McMurtry's central theme is the unifying thread between Thalia and Houston. The people of the novels — from *Horseman, Pass By* and *The Last Picture Show* to the Houston trilogy — are actors in a massive Texas drama. Victims of time and place, they must deal with a world in transition, in which they have few guides and over which they have no control.

3   Houston: The Second Literary Home

The next group of three novels, all set in Houston, grew out of McMurtry's urban experience. Although not as intimate with this city as with Archer City, McMurtry was attracted to Houston; its hodgepodge of *nouveaux riches,* country-bred workers, poor folks, and young adults intrigued him. To McMurtry, Houston was a female deciding what kind of woman she would become. Would she be "a penny-clutching widow"? Or would she "with her money and sexy trees" be a kind of mother city that would "attract and accept the sort of imagination that could bring her to a rich maturity"? He muses further about the city's future: "Her children might be interesting to know. They will be natural urbanites, most of them, members of the first generation of Texans to belong in fact and in spirit to a fertile city, not to the Old Man of the country or the Old Maid of the towns." [1]

In the 1960s, however, many of her young adults were refugees from the dying countryside, and McMurtry wanted to use their relocation as a central problem in his next works. His earlier novels had dealt with the effects of change on a rural region and its inhabitants. His next three shifted concern to the effects of living in a new environment, for he knew that "the pressures in Dallas and Houston can destroy or at least radically alter a rural orientation within a few years." [2] Despite their many fine passages, McMurtry's urban novels reveal tension between the author's urge to write about the "part ridiculous and part tragic" movement from "homeplace to metropolis" and his lack of inspiration.

Urban fiction was not McMurtry's natural genre. Despite his familiarity with the city, he realized that cities "apparently failed to seed" the "imagination with those pregnant images from which a living and well-voiced fiction might grow." He says of himself and other Texas novelists, "We are country writers yet, but country writers who have moved to the city to write. . . . The emotions, images, symbols that animate our books pertain to the country still." The move to the city had not provided McMurtry with enough stimulus either; to him Texas cities were hardly any more tolerant of thinkers than the rural region had been. Set apart from society, Texas writers became "symbolic frontiersmen . . . attempting to keep the frontiersman's sense of daring and independence by seeking these qualities, not in the life of action but in the life of the mind. It is still daring enough, in Texas, to commit oneself to the life of the mind, and it is our only corollary to that other kind of daring — a kind that has small place in this land of cities." [3] McMurtry's "daring life" in Texas soon ended.

In A Narrow Grave was McMurtry's farewell. In 1969 he left Texas for the Virginia countryside near Washington. He did not return for five years. Soon after this relocation, he finished *Moving On*. Writing the novel had been difficult, and McMurtry expressed doubts whether he had "any business setting a novel in any city, Texan or otherwise." [4] His manuscript, started at least as early as 1964, went through three or four titles, versions, and changes in point of view. [5] *Moving On* is a 794-page *Bildungsroman,* set primarily in Houston, narrating the marriage and divorce of Patsy Carpenter, an intelligent and attractive young woman who leads a tearful, aimless life. Even her emotional emancipation at the novel's end is tenuous. In her wanderings Patsy encounters dozens of people representing the gamut of Texas society: rodeo performers, oil-wealthy social elites, old cattlemen, university intellectuals, and hippie dropouts.

Moving On is the first novel of the Houston trilogy, three books set between 1961 and 1976 which relate the early adulthood of three Houston young people — Patsy Carpenter in *Moving On* (1970), Danny Deck in *All My Friends Are Going to Be Strangers* (1972), and Emma Horton in *Terms of Endearment* (1975). McMurtry stated that he intended the trilogy to be about couples: "The novels are just filled with couples, all kinds." He was most interested in "a set of perspectives on marriage and couples." [6] The theme of the trilogy extends, however, beyond unhappy marriages to other emotional crises. All strata of urban society suffer from loneliness, confusion, apathy, and disorientation.

Although writing *Moving On* was difficult, the next novel came easily. McMurtry feels that *"All My Friends* is a lucky book, in that I wrote it after *Moving On*, and I was quite tired, but I had a sort of momentum going, and I thought: I might just do a quick book." Because it was written rapidly, "it has an unself-conscious tone that I probably could not have got if I had tried. I'm really happy with it." [7] The novel is a modern picaresque, the story of a Rice University student-writer rambling around Texas and California and falling innocently into and out of a number of sexual adventures. Narrated by the guileless protagonist Danny Deck, this rather plotless novel is held together by the innocent charm of Danny's voice.

Bookish and gifted, Danny is nonetheless just as provincial and undirected as Lonnie Bannon and Sonny Crawford. In fact, Danny's grandparents lived on Idiot Ridge, the site of the Bannon homestead, and the intelligentsia Danny socializes with in Austin and Houston ridicules that fact. They call him a "frontier genius" with none of the manners of the cultivated class; instead, he has body odor, unkempt hair, and notorious drinking habits. Danny's father was a small-town Pontiac dealer who considered this son a black sheep in the family. The boy had never flown in a plane nor been to nearby Louisiana. No one in his family had approved of his extensive reading. Perhaps because of his restricted youth, Danny lacks confidence and feels guilty and depressed. He never adjusts to having money. Even with a bank account of $40,000, he lives like a vagabond.

Danny is hardly capable of taking care of himself emotionally. He falls in love easily and completely and excuses his attraction to Sally Bynum by explaining, "I had given myself over and had no mechanism for taking myself back." [8] He continually makes unwise decisions, like marrying Sally, partly because he has no family for support or advice. His mother is dead and his father too busy. He bumbles his way into and out of human relationships, especially with women. Toward the end of the novel, Danny realizes, "My fate seemed to be to meet women it was impossible not to love, but whom it was also impossible to love right" (253).

Danny's impulsive marriage to Sally and the acceptance of his novel for publication upset what stability college routines had provided. This new phase in Danny's life is too unsettling: "I didn't fit it any more," he notes after a disastrous party at a professor's house. "All the furniture of my life had been changed around. . . . Without wanting it to happen, I had let myself be dislodged. Dislodged was exactly how I felt" (59–60). Danny feels he must leave Houston. He and Sally then move to California, where their marriage dissolves, and Danny finds himself increasingly depressed by his uprooting. Several affairs momentarily relieve his depression, but even they, for one reason or another, never satisfy. Eventually, after completing his second novel, Danny returns to Texas to claim his child and to visit old friends. As the novel's title suggests, those experiences are abortive: Danny's emotional outburst at Sally's parents hopelessly alienates him from his infant daughter, and his one-night affair with Emma upsets his friendship with her and her husband. In despair, he leaves Houston a second time and heads toward Mexico. In the end, Danny, tired and depressed and intoxicated, wades into the Rio Grande to drown his manuscript.

Danny Deck is, in many ways, Larry McMurtry, the young writer of *Horseman, Pass By*. Danny's first novel had been completed, like McMurtry's, when he was a Rice student. Both character and creator were essentially country boys surprised to be "real" writers, not just students writing stories. Although the tone of McMurtry's letters written while he was a student is certainly more sophisticated than Danny's narration, both McMurtry and Danny appear as shy young men who love books but also enjoy being with people.[9] Both spent several months in San Francisco and were there when their books — which had similar plots — were published in 1961. Danny's novel, *The Restless Grass,* narrates the life of an old man with two sons, one good and one bad. The novel is the same length as *Horseman, Pass By*. Danny acquires McMurtry's writing habits and attitudes about writing even though he is characteristically less emphatic: "It was true that I got up and wrote for a couple of hours every morning," Danny says, "but I had never thought of that as discipline. . . . In fact, I liked to get up early. I liked writing, too — at least I usually liked it." [10]

McMurtry is generally reticent about personal feelings, but Danny's emotional conflicts echo McMurtry's own attitudes toward Houston, rural heritage, and writing. Danny's thoughts the night he exiles himself from the city eloquently explain the attraction he and McMurtry felt for *her:*

> Houston was my companion on the walk. She had been my mistress, but after a thousand nights together, just the two of us, we were calling it off. It was a warm, moist, mushy, smelly night, the way her best nights were. The things most people hated about her were the things I loved: her heat, her dampness, her sumpy smells. She wasn't beautiful, but neither was I. I liked her heat and her looseness and her smells. . . . I could still love her. (62–63)

Danny finds not only Houston difficult to abandon; Texas also seems to hold him as he drives west past El Paso. "It was strange, leaving Texas. . . . It was all behind me, north to south, not lying there exactly, but more like looming there over the car, not a state or a stretch of land but some giant, some genie, some god, towering over the road" (82). Danny lives in San Francisco many months and never really makes her acquaintance — "like two people who notice each other at a party but never get to talk" (170). When Danny returns to Texas, he realizes that out of the state he lacked sensitivity, a feeling for the world:

> It was the sky that was Texas, the sky that welcomed me back. The land I didn't care for all that much — it was bleak and monotonous and full of ugly little towns. The sky was what I had been missing, and seeing it again in its morning brightness made me realize suddenly why I hadn't been myself for many months. It had such depth and such spaciousness and such incredible compass, it took so much in and circled one with such a tremendous generous space that it was impossible not to feel more intensely with it above you. (176)

Once Danny is in Texas again, however, the McMurtry ambivalence toward the state recurs. Not too far into his cross-state trek Danny visits the bizarre ranch of his Uncle Laredo, a ninety-two-year-old rancher living on god-forsaken land south of Van Horn. Uncle L has recently married an elderly but formidable neighbor whom he regularly visits just for supper. The half-crazy

old man and his Mexican cook live a wretched life, eating and
sleeping around a campfire and never using the ranch house, a
four-story Gothic structure, built by an English architect who later
died when he and his mistress jumped from the mansion's fourth-
story porch.

The episode at Uncle Laredo's ranch is a parody of *Horseman,
Pass By,* a bitter re-creation of the Western experience in Mc-
Murtry's fiction. Uncle L's attitude toward the land is dramati-
cally opposed to Homer Bannon's. Danny's uncle stabs the earth
with a crowbar, ostensibly making hundreds of postholes, but
Danny feels he does it "because he hated the earth and wanted to
get in as many licks at it as he could before he died" (180).

Uncle Laredo is patterned on McMurtry's Uncle Johnny,
whose house "was a towering three story edifice . . . built by an extremely eccentric New York architect" whose wife drove him mad.
Eventually, the architect killed his wife in the mansion and the
blood on the carpet remained for the McMurtry family to see.
"Nothing," the novelist remembers, "could have had a more Dos-
toevskian impact on such simple Texas kids as we were than that
large irregular stain on the basement rug." [11] Uncle Laredo's sleeping habits, hired help, and marriage are only slight exaggerations of
Uncle Johnny's peculiar life. The uncles also share the same attitude toward their writer-nephews. As a hired hand, Danny
"wouldn't be worth a shit," Uncle L proclaims. "All he's ever done
is read" (197).

Danny's experience with Uncle Laredo abruptly washes away
his sentimental mood. "The Hacienda of the Bitter Waters wasn't
the Old West I liked to believe in — it was the bitter end of something. I knew I would never want to visit it again" (199). After this
episode, neither Danny nor any of McMurtry's other characters
appear in a Western setting for many years.

As Danny continues across Texas, he recalls the place of his
origins, the place from which he has banished himself: "Three
hundred miles to the north was Idiot Ridge, where Granny Deck
had lived and died. It was just a little bluff, with lots of mesquite
trees and rattlesnakes, but," he adds significantly, "in a way it was
the place most truly mine. The ridge was the northern boundary of
a valley called the Sorrows, which my mean old grandfather had
homesteaded with his first wife" (212).

Since leaving San Francisco, Danny has been haunted by the

stories of his people. He remembers how his grandfather bartered skunk hides for Granny Deck, his second wife. He remembers the pathetic tale of Old Man Goodnight giving a ragged band of Indians a buffalo to kill, not for food but for one final chase. In the Salinas Valley fog Danny imagines spirits emerging from the whiteness and wants to "talk with Granny and Old Man Goodnight and ask them if I had their stories right" (174). But once he gets to Texas, Danny is reluctant to publish their stories: "I didn't want to tell the world about the sadness of Granny, as she sat in a flapping tent in the 1880s, listening to Grandpa count out skunk hides. I didn't want to tell about the sadness of the Indians, as they sat watching the buffalo grunt out its last grunts" (213).

These stories form the prologue and epilogue of a novel Danny abandons while in California in favor of a more pertinent story, one about itinerant young couples who "were a great interlocking swirl of lovers and boyfriends and mistresses, ex-mistresses, wives, ex-wives" (142). This second novel, "The Man Who Never Learned," is like those in McMurtry's Houston trilogy. At the end of *All My Friends Are Going to Be Strangers*, Danny takes curious but not surprising action. Rivers fascinate Danny. He had read and reread river books and wanted to see the great rivers of the world. When his return to Houston turns into a fiasco, he heads instinctively toward the Rio Grande, for "it was always a borderland I had lived on . . . a thin little strip between the country of the normal and the country of the strange. Perhaps my true country was the borderland, anyway" (285). By now his California novel offers no comfort. "Pages. Words. Black marks on paper. They didn't have eyes, or bodies. They weren't people. I didn't know why I put marks on paper" (278).

Just before Danny destroys the manuscript in the river, however, he pulls out his old prologue and epilogue. "Granny and Old Man Goodnight were the only good things in the box. Emma might like them" (283). Danny then disappears, but his presence haunts three future McMurtry novels. And his Old West stories, McMurtry's stories, appear years later in *Lonesome Dove* (1985).

McMurtry has often minimized the problems he faces as a writer. In an interview with Patrick Bennett, he commented that he likes writing, balances his time with his other vocation as a rare book dealer, and never suffers much in writing fiction.[12] *All My Friends Are Going to Be Strangers* depicts a dark side of McMurtry's writing, however. When Danny learns that his novel will be published, he somewhat vaguely notes, "I had got one dream but something felt wrong in the pit of my stomach. Maybe some other dream was being taken away from me forever. Maybe I wanted that one more" (22). In California he realizes that writers are not so rare as Texans think. He meets dozens of writers and realizes that if he is going to "be good enough to count," he would need to become ten times better than he was (85).

With this new insight Danny questions whether or not he should continue to write but decides that he "would have to keep writing out of pride," until he was "good enough at it to be able to quit" (114). Later on, Danny feels more confident and determined:

> I probably *was* a real writer. If I kept at it I could probably write as good as anybody but the geniuses. I could be better than average. I could probably even be minor. With great luck I might, by accident mostly, write something fine, sometime in my life, particularly if I kept myself in shape by writing books that were decently good for twenty years or so. (231)

Writing, however, will never bring Danny happiness or friends. McMurtry commented that Danny realizes that some relationship exists "between writing and life, and that it is not clear-cut. He has some sense at the end of the book that it is hopeless, that either he won't be much of a writer, or that the better he writes, somehow, the more it's going to alienate him." [13]

McMurtry claims that this emotional crisis is the only autobiographical element in *All My Friends Are Going to Be Strangers:*

> It is true that the better you write the worse you live. The more of yourself you take out of real relationships and project into fantasy relationships the more the real relationships suffer. The popular theory is that writing grows out of a neurosis, and is a cure for neurosis. This is nonsense. It may grow out of neurosis, but it doesn't cure it; if anything, it drives it deeper and makes it nearer to being psychosis. I do not think that *real* writing is a purgative, though there must be some people who let off tensions by writing. I do not think that writing, or any art, pursued seriously, is necessarily a health producing activity. Writing involves a kind of gambling with the subconscious and the destruction of self-defenses. [14]

Danny lacked self-defense mechanisms to protect his mental health, but McMurtry was no longer Danny Deck. The creator of Danny understood that memories haunt and writing alienates, and as he matured, McMurtry worked to construct defenses. Meanwhile, his next novel was another gamble with personal feelings.

Terms of Endearment, published in 1975, was originally intended as Emma's book. Emma Horton had been present as Patsy's best friend in *Moving On* and as Danny's good friend and devoted fan in *All My Friends Are Going to Be Strangers.* In the final version of *Terms of Endearment,* however, she is again subordinate to the main character. Emma's mother, Aurora Greenway, takes over the novel in the same charming and aggressive way she takes over everything else. Only the last fifth of this novel, an abrupt addendum to the Houston trilogy, set in the Midwest nine to fourteen years later, is truly Emma's story.

By the time *Terms of Endearment* was complete, McMurtry was almost forty years old. Young people were no longer his primary concern, and the problems of aging were increasingly more relevant. Emma's own story is developed when she reaches her mid-thirties. *Terms of Endearment* narrates the story of older men and women, past their prime but still feeling the emotions of younger people. The first section, "Emma's Mother," is a novelistic comedy of manners. Aurora's bantering and outrageous attitudes produce delightful witticisms and absurdities. Texas poet R. G. Vliet wrote that he could not "think of a more accomplished comedy of manners piece in modern fiction outside of the work of Evelyn Waugh" and praised McMurtry's use of language in this novel. Vliet notes especially McMurtry's exploitation of frontier invective "still alive in the social exchange of contemporary Texans" as well as his use of formal language required in a comedy of manners, accomplished "without bringing attention to it at all." [15]

In "Emma's Mother," McMurtry distances himself from the material. Consequently, the novel lacks characteristic McMurtry poignancy but gains delightful scintillation. *Terms of Endearment* also exhibits McMurtry's versatility in social setting. Scenes of male-female conflict range from Aurora's dumping pompano on the table of the best French restaurant in Houston to Royce Dunlap's running down the East-Tex Hoedown in his baby-blue potato chip delivery truck. Despite this new tone and emphasis, however, *Terms of Endearment* retains an old McMurtry theme — the plight of individuals when their world changes.

As characters like Emma and Aurora confirm, McMurtry obviously has much more admiration for modern urban women than he has for urban men. Emma is by his own admission a favorite character.[16] Fat and frumpy, she is also warm-hearted, tolerant, and devoted, despite her marital disappointments. Her intelligence is restricted by her unimaginative husband and her own lack of ambition. She copes with her repressed life through lethargy, a tendency easily enhanced by Houston's omnipresent heat. She would "suspend" herself in a state between sleep and daydreaming in her hot garage apartment. "When she really didn't know what to do with herself, she had learned to do nothing at all." [17] Emma represents the bright young people McMurtry knew in graduate school in the 1950s and early 1960s. These students were "a class of people who were going to develop tastes beyond their means. They were educated and they were sensitive and they knew a lot, but they didn't have a lot" — nor would they likely ever have much.[18]

No matter where the Hortons live, their marriage is uninspired, even destructive. Never overly productive, Flap eventually becomes a tenured failure at a small Midwestern college. He blames his fruitless career on Emma because she would not push him. In truth, she does not want a truly successful husband since ambition would further alienate their family life. Emma hopes in vain "for some middle ground" on which Flap could be "friendly and relaxed and incline him to stay at home a little" (366). Emma's last years, narrated in "Mrs. Greenway's Daughter," are not unlike Danny Deck's last months. She falls into a number of affairs, but none of them produces much happiness. She never acquires her mother's flair for living, and finally Aurora admits that her daughter would have been "a little happier if she had been . . . faintly ridiculous . . . too" (410).

Aurora is altogether a different woman. Flamboyant and ridiculous, she functions best in her home that is, in fact, an extension of herself: "The house was too lovely, too comfortable, too much hers — her furniture, her kitchen, her yard and her flowers and her birds, her patio and her window nook. Without them she would not merely have to change, she would have to find another person to be" (148). Fortified with her house and her exuberance, she develops opinions and habits which become tactics for fending off age. Aurora fights against dullness in herself and all those around her, but underneath the gaiety she is deeply concerned about her future and fearful of loneliness.

Rosie Dunlap, Aurora's maid from Shreveport, Louisiana, is in every way her boss's opposite. While Aurora is buxom, happy, rich, and lazy, Rosie is skinny, miserable, poor, hardworking. They fuss continually, but in their opinion of men they agree. Even though Rosie warns Aurora not to criticize the Dunlaps' ne'er-do-well children because "I'll light into you like a rat terrier, first thing you know," the fiesty little maid readily criticizes Emma's marriage: "She's got a heavy cross to bear. That sickly dog of a husband of hers ain't fit to kick off the porch" (47–48). McMurtry apparently shares Rosie and Aurora's opinion of men. He admits, in fact, that he likes women more than men. In an interview with Maureen Orth, he commented, "I always wondered why women put up with men, to tell the truth." His women characters "tend to put up with drips and creeps. But that happens very frequently in life. . . . Most of the women I know," he continued, "are very tenacious in their affections — far more than most men . . . because they retain some intrinsic hopefulness longer than men do." [19]

The men in the lives of Emma, Rosie, and Aurora confirm this assertion. Emma's husband and lovers — including Danny Deck — are ineffectual and misdirected. Rosie's Royce is nothing more than a dumb, beer-sipping delivery man easily dominated by his girlfriend Shirl. Aurora's suitors are, with one exception, has-beens. Hector has been a four-star general who commanded a tank division; Alberto, a famous Genoan opera star; and Trevor, a wealthy playboy from the East Coast. At this point in their lives, however, they appear little more than old fools hopelessly pursuing Aurora.

In *Terms of Endearment* McMurtry creates major characters who are not native Texans. Aurora and most of her suitors are natural urbanites from around the world, and they are "interesting to know." McMurtry's most unique creation in the novel is, however, a Texan — and a symbolic frontiersman. Vernon Dalhart's major attribute is "wheelerdealerism," which McMurtry views as "an extension of the frontier ethos, refined and transplanted to an urban context." [20] An eccentric and benevolent oil millionaire, Vernon, who can arrange anything, is the modern equivalent of the old-time, gallant cattleman. Vernon's horse and home is a long white Lincoln equipped with telephone, icebox, and television, and his range is the vast world of the oil industry. Vernon enjoys his place above the streets of Houston because "he could see so far, literally, that in his mind's eye he could often see the places he was calling:

Amarillo or Midland, the Gulf shore, Caracas or Bogota" (157–158). His customized car and a little nightly niche on the top floor of his parking garage were the only things "money had bought him that he loved completely and never tired of" — until he meets Aurora. Unfortunately, fifty-year-old Vernon has never had time for women. Although his efficiency and energy leave all other characters, except Rosie, standing still, he lacks the assertiveness to win Aurora and the experience to understand her assaults and moods.

McMurtry also addresses the issue of the frontier spirit in his humorous renditions of Houston's violence. Social frustrations, not jealousy, are the ultimate reasons why Royce Dunlap crashes his truck into the dance floor at the East-Tex Hoedown and why Mitch McDonald assaults Royce with a machete. "A great many Houstonians are still in the process of transition from country ways to city ways," he explains in *In A Narrow Grave*. "Many of them are poor, and the unaccustomed urban pressures frustrate them severely. To let off steam they go to honky-tonks. . . . In such a place, with a little beer under his belt, a man is apt to find that his frustrations are uncontainable." [21]

Transition affects parent and child, man and wife. Male-female roles continue to metamorphose as families move from the land to the small towns and, finally, to the cities. McMurtry's women feel their husbands' indifference toward marriage. Rosie laments her husband's apathy as she heads into an emotional breakdown. Emma too feels Flap is no longer sensitive to her needs. On the frontier, men had dominated, but in McMurtry's city they generally lose their forcefulness and are transformed into frustrated and inept husbands and lovers.

Given this situation, women characters, who are intelligent and capable, assume responsibility for whatever institutions are in crisis, especially marriages. *Terms of Endearment* opens with Aurora's advice to Emma, "The success of a marriage invariably depends on the woman" (11), and it ends at Emma's funeral as Aurora and Patsy, the two survivors of the Houston trilogy, leave the grave. Shouldering their responsibility and grief, "they turned and went to attend to the children and the men" (410).

Emma dies, Danny disappears, and Patsy reestablishes herself on the West Coast. McMurtry's characters vanish from the state, just as he did. He cannot, however, dismiss these characters easily, and for that purpose the second part of *Terms of Endearment* seems to have been written. It is a separate story, a tying of loose ends. Emma follows Flap to the Midwest and eventually develops cancer at the age of thirty-seven. The fate of Emma, a touchstone for three novels, seems too much for McMurtry, for her death is extended and maudlin. Perhaps he shared Danny Deck's emotions here as well. "My heart was with the people in *The Man Who Never Learned*," Danny states as he completes that novel. "They were alive, to me. I didn't want to stop writing about them, or knowing them" (167–168).

Since characters in *Terms of Endearment* must reconcile themselves with Emma's fate, emotions treated lightly in the first section suddenly become serious human feelings — the love of mother and daughter, mother and children, friends and friends. Emma's own thoughts as she slowly dies affirm humanity's essential need for love. Her son Teddy "needed arms around him, ears to listen; he needed everyone in the house to be warmly, constantly in love with one another." Teddy's yearnings "haunted her" (365). In her last days Emma examines her alienated husband and sees his old arrogant look. "Somehow that look had won her, though she couldn't remember, looking at him, what the terms of endearment had been, or how they had been lost for so long" (400). This regretful mood extends to ten years later when Flap remembers Emma and feels "that he had done something wrong, wrong, wrong, long ago" (401).

In Emma's last conscious days, McMurtry presents a kind of final reconciliation between his two favorite characters. One of Emma's last requests is to have her copy of Danny's novel, and she keeps it by her side. "As she slowly began to forget her life, his memory returned. In her dreams they began to have conversations, though she could never remember where they had talked or what they said" (408).

Perhaps, as McMurtry exiled himself from Texas, the characters in his fictional world became more and more a part of him, substitutes for the imaginative seed the frontier had sown in his youth. Characters became more important than place in the Houston trilogy. No longer do McMurtry's novels speak of a particular place; instead Aurora Greenway and Emma Horton's novel could be set in any American city. But characters, like place, must be forgotten. He tends to kill his creations fictionally and emotionally, to drown them in a river as Danny Deck had done to his characters.

Emma and Danny are somehow saved from this exorcism. Perhaps they — like the frontier myth — are too much a part of

McMurtry to dismiss completely. The novelist quickly berates his other works. Only *Terms of Endearment* and *All My Friends Are Going to Be Strangers* remain tolerable novels: "the only two that I can stand to think about at all." [22] Rejection of his written work is one mechanism McMurtry uses to cope with the self-destruction of creating fiction. Now, with Texas denounced and with the Houston trilogy over, McMurtry began again searching for fictional worlds, for new inspiration. Meanwhile, the old prologue and epilogue that Danny had sent Emma existed in some closet, somewhere.

4   Searching for a New Home

The characters in McMurtry's first six novels experience change of setting. These transformations generate loss and confusion in stories that echo McMurtry's life. Born to a frontier family who revered a dying way of life, McMurtry left, but has never quite dismissed his heritage. Even the home he chose as an adult, though attractive in many ways, was eventually too restricting. In the next three novels McMurtry attempts to free himself from geographical confinement and experiments with different settings. Although Texas is not ignored altogether, the state becomes less consequential in each consecutive book. Taken as a whole, these novels present a writer wandering in search of a new home for his restless and inquiring mind.

The wandering motif occurs early in the Houston trilogy. Drives across the Midwest and West structure much of the story in *Moving On* and *All My Friends Are Going to Be Strangers*. Patsy and Danny never appear to be pursuing a single quest; rather, they enjoy wandering for its own sake. In a sense they are trying to arrive at that culminating scene which McMurtry first envisioned, the scene that generated the rest of the novel. The process, however, is painful for them and unpredictable for their creator.[1] The moods and actions of McMurtry's characters are determined by where they are, and generally they become disoriented in all but the most familiar surroundings, even when they initiate the change. Lonnie and Sonny feel lost and lonely as their region changes. Danny at his typewriter table and Emma in her kitchen are comfortable and productive, but away from those settings they flounder.

After completing the Houston novels, McMurtry sought other settings for his fiction. He felt he could no longer write about Texas because he was no longer a part of it. He did not even visit the state from 1969 to 1974. In an essay written for *Atlantic Monthly* in 1975, the year *Terms of Endearment* was published, he declared that "the only way to know one's home is to live in it — if one doesn't want to live in a state, it is really fanciful to call it home. Intimacy with a place is not to be had at any lighter price than intimacy with a person . . . and infrequent visits do not preserve it." [2] McMurtry dismissed the entire state as articulately as he had the rural experience several years earlier. To McMurtry, Texas had become as intellectually stagnating as Archer City had been when he was a youth. "For people with active intellective needs," he claimed, "the state becomes increasingly less habitable as they mature and these needs increase. Informed conversation is simply too hard to get; those who could give it are spread too thin." The move was also made in order that he might find new fictional worlds:

> I got tired of dealing creatively with the kind of mental and emotive inarticulatenes that I found in Texas. The move off the land is now virtually completed, and that was the great subject that Texas offered writers of my generation. The one basic subject it offers us now is loneliness, and one can only ring the changes on that so many times.[3]

For his next subject, then, McMurtry chose a completely new setting — Hollywood, a city he had been acquainted with since the early 1960s.

McMurtry's title character was Jill Peel, a Hollywood cartoonist who had been Danny Deck's California lover. Several characters in *Somebody's Darling*, published in 1978, appear in the Houston trilogy, and the novel is, in a way, an extension of that series, set in California a decade or so later. It pursues one of McMurtry's primary interests — development of characters through time. McMurtry has commented that he, like nineteenth-century novelists, enjoys the ability to "convey the passage of time, moving people from generation to generation, or at least decade to decade. Consequently it is very appealing to be able to take a character and carry him through more than one book, or to pick up a character who is a minor character in one book and give him a book of his own." [4]

Somebody's Darling, structured in three parts and told from three points of view, narrates the successful career and unhappy loves of cartoonist-director Jill Peel. Only the first section, told from the point of view of an aging but gallant Fitzgerald-like screenwriter, reads credibly. McMurtry himself "wasn't really stirred by it, even as I went along," partially because he had waited too long to write the novel. "It never came up to the vision I had of it long before I tried to write it." [5] The experience was instructive, however, since McMurtry then realized the perils of finding new settings. He admitted that even though quite familiar with Los Angeles, he did not "have the depth of reference for it, and I didn't have the depth or the complexity of feeling for it; and I think it's the latter quality that is most important." [6] Some of the ideas expressed in the *Atlantic Monthly* article were revised, for writing *Somebody's Darling* altered his perspective on place. Although he still rejected further Texas material, he realized what Southern writers especially had long known — memories generate powerful emotions. A writer needs to feel a place more than live it. He told one audience in 1978:

> Not only do you need to know the place that you write about very, very well, but you need to feel something, something deep for it, not necessarily simple love, . . . not necessarily total admiration of the boosteristic sort, but something deep, something that is a mixture of emotions, perhaps a love-hate relationship. . . . Something deep enough that will lead you to the stories that, set in a particular context of your place, will allow you to use your talent to the fullest to illuminate the human condition, problems of the human condition. [7]

Thus, after completing *Somebody's Darling,* McMurtry was in even more of a dilemma than he had been after finishing the Houston trilogy. He had "pretty well covered the spectrum of Texas" as he knew it and even "made the foolish effort to write a book about Los Angeles." And now he wondered what book he would write next. [8]

Four years later, in 1982, the next novel appeared. *Cadillac Jack* was inspired by twelve years of experience in Washington, D.C., and by twenty years of experience as a book scout. Narrated by a middle-aged picaro, the book relates the adventures of an antiques scout from Texas who roams the country in search of extraordinary objects and beautiful women. The novel finds Jack McGriff in Washington, not prepared for what he experiences. Although completely out of place among the capital's social elite, Jack, who looks like a tall, over-dressed cowboy, is generally admired. His discomfort in Washington society never lasts too long because his home, "a pearl-covered Cadillac with peach velour interior," [9] is always parked nearby for a getaway onto the highways of America, where he is happiest.

McMurtry recognized that as a writer he lacked the depth of feeling for Washington to create a truly emotive story, so he turned to the light satire he felt appropriate for this setting. *"Cadillac Jack* is a mock epic," he explains. "Since Washington tends to a kind of eighteenth-century manners, I thought it should be treated in the eighteenth-century form — the mock epic." [10] Washington society is portrayed as both dull and bizarre. The novel opens as one renowned hostess, Pencil Penrose, sets her pet pugs on the dinner table. "I was frankly shocked," Jack narrates. "I had eaten at a number of tables where it was customary to set the plates under the table for the dogs, but never at one where the dogs were put on the table and given a go at the plates" (46).

Washington hides a number of eccentrics and colorful characters, but freewheeling Jack finds it generally dull and gray:

> Already I was getting the sense that Washington was a very cellular place. The motif of the cell recurred. All the men in trench coats and woolen hats probably spent their days in cell-like offices in vast gray buildings. Then when the government let them out they squirmed like larvae into small cell-like cars and rushed across the river or around the Beltway to vast gray apartment buildings, where they inhabited cell-like apartments.
>
> During the day, in their cell-like offices, they probably spent their time hatching plots the size of microscopic organisms. (123)

Those inhabitants of the city not part of its wormy world eagerly seek divertissement in any form, including espionage, sex, and nest collecting. [11]

Cadillac Jack satirizes popular culture's adoration of Texas. Using this fascination as a selling tactic, Jack the antiques scout persuades his chic girlfriend Cindy to buy and display used cowboy boots in her art gallery. As critic Don Graham points out, "The novel ends with a scene at a new boutique in fashionable George-town, where rich society and media celebrities gather to ogle au-thentic cowboy boots amidst an array of cowboy poseurs, presided over by native son and anchorman, Dan Rather." [12]

While celebrities seem somewhat ridiculous admiring cowboy-ana, the real Texans in the novel comfortably and successfully pur-sue other interests. Boog Miller, stereotypical Texas politician, is rich, crude, and surprisingly intelligent. A true wheeler-dealer, reminiscent of the LBJ era, Boog demonstrates how Texan self-re-liance, energy, and cunning can quickly manipulate the nation's duller citizens.

Strange people clutter *Cadillac Jack* just as strange objects clut-ter junk shops and collectors' homes that Jack visits. At one point in the novel, Jack sits in a Safeway parking lot watching "a garden of grotesques," poor, stooped people who like Jack are "slightly off center" (242). The entire novel, as a matter of fact, cultivates a weedy garden of grotesques — eccentric collectors and multimil-lionaires, Washington journalists and politicians with names like Dunscombe and Cunard Cotswinkle, Moorcock Malone, Lilah Landry, Khaki Descartes, Sir Cripps Crisp, Spud Breyfogle, and George Psalmanazar — who function as a bizarre backdrop for the central story of Jack's entanglement with objects and women.

Married twice and in love many times, Jack usually finds him-self powerless against females. "Every single time I've gone one-on-one with female defiance, I've ended up face down on the floor, twitching weakly," he laments. "One thing I've learned to do with-out is the myth of male dominance. Possibly there had actually been male dominance in other eras, but constant exposure to women on the order of Boss Miller and Tanya Todd convinced me it had gone the way of the dodo and the greak auk" (33).

Cindy Sanders and Jean Arber are Jack's Washington inter-ests. Cindy, Jack knows, is a totally selfish social climber, but she is extraordinarily beautiful, and Jack appreciates rare beauty in women as well as in the objects he finds. Jean, a more attractive and spirited version of Emma Horton, seems to be the novel's one normal character. Mother of two delightful girls and only recently separated from her husband, Jean "didn't seem quite equal to the outside world" where she had just established an antiques busi-ness. "But in her own kitchen," Jack admits, "she seemed more than equal, both to the world and to me" (247). Jean's three-year-old daughter is always in control, always dominating her family and Jack. McMurtry admits fascination with little females. "I love argumentative, articulate little girls. They're charming. It's interesting to see how early in some cases a female will begin to operate with a consciousness of feminine power." [13]

Jack's women in Texas, including two ex-wives, never appear in the novel. Instead, they have blended into their Texas setting:

> Their qualities and the qualities of their three cities were very similar, their rhythms the rhythms of those places. To the extent that I understood the places, I understood the women, and vice versa.
>
> Nothing like that applied to my relationship in the District of Columbia and its environs, where I understood nothing, neither the women nor the place. (313)

The Washington females Jack encounters are remembered in more limited settings. Since they do not fit the city's dull patterns, their interesting qualities come from their own created environments, Cindy's boutique and Jean's kitchen.

Much of Jack's Texas background recalls McMurtry's earlier protagonists. Jack was a poor boy who grew up in a trailer house in a small South Texas town. His mother died early, and his father "took little part" in his life. He flatly states that for his father "clerking in the local hardware store was good enough . . . and still is" (23). Jack, however, is the ultimate roamer, a fantasy male. Once a college basketball star and later a world-champion bull-dogger, Jack became rich with a lucky find in DeQueen, Arkansas.

Before visiting Washington, Jack was confident of his passions, enjoyed taking and leaving, buying and selling. "I buy and sell as I go, seldom keeping anything more than a week or two," he rather offhandedly brags. "My kind of buying is like my kind of falling in love: a matter of immediate eye appeal. I fall in love with objects, each in its turn, my only problem being that as I get older I also get pickier" (12–13). Once he gets to Washington, Jack's capacity for wanting expands. Suddenly, he wants several women and a great many things (102). He has possessed discipline "right up until the moment" he met Cindy (312–313). Now, at the age of thirty-three, he almost resorts to adolescent behavior. With Cindy he reaches "the acme of something: the boy, from the little cowtown in the West," with his daydream, "the homecoming queen from the far Pacific shore" (56).[14]

Eventually, though, Jack tires of all objects, suddenly loses his "appetite for the bizarre," and "O.D.ed on objects" (234). Sensible Jean realizes that the change is probably temporary, that he will never truly reform or mature. When he proposes to her, she replies:

> You don't want to love anyone a lot. . . . It's tiresome work. Means holding still and being bored half the time. I think you'd just rather move around collecting little loves. Affections. Little light ones that you can put in your car for a while and then get rid of. (386)

Cadillac Jack portrays people who fear deep commitments, and it ridicules America's materialistic passion for whatever is attainable. Jack observes rather cynically, "People imbued from childhood with the myth of the primacy of feeling seldom like to admit they really want *things* as much as they might want love, but my career has convinced me that plenty of them do. And some want things a lot worse than they want love" (86).

Obviously, Jack's experiences at estate sales, flea markets, and garage sales draw on McMurtry's own years as a rare book scout, a vocation almost as important to him as writing. Jack's roaming spirit also belongs to McMurtry, for the novelist once estimated that he spent one hundred nights a year on the road.[15] Like Mc-Murtry, Jack loves a big car and the open road. In fact, the hero joined the rodeo circuit in his earlier days for "the opportunity . . . to drive across vast, lonely American spaces" (25). The sky especially attracts Jack, just as it did Danny Deck: "America itself was very beautiful, very various. . . . The skies over the west were so lovely that they alone should have been enough to sustain me" (364). Most significantly, however, Jack is troubled by his past. He may be eccentric, but some self-defense mechanism saves him from being neurotic. Memories come in the form of a frequent dream in which he is driving backward[16] through his life:

> As the dream progresses the cuts get faster and I regress through ten years of cars, back at least to the GMC pickup I used during my first year on the rodeo circuit. The roads get worse, too — often I find myself zooming backward over the gritty wastes near Monahans, Texas, before the little psychic balance bar that keeps me from becoming an insane person tilts me back toward wakefulness. (19)

McMurtry gives Jack indifference and mental discipline, two characteristics Danny Deck lacks. Consequently, the earlier hero is vulnerable and emotional with no mechanism for bringing himself out of crises, while Jack continues through life unattached.

Jack has reached a time when he is not easily satisfied, and he fears above all that he is "looking downward from a peak" (27). Twice in his life, once when he threw a steer in a record-breaking 4.1 seconds and again when he found an extraordinary Sung vase in Mom and Pop Cullin's junk barn, he "shot up and over a peak," and now he "could expect to work the down side of the hill for several months or years" (14). This expectation is a middle-aged and professional concern. McMurtry himself must have wondered, after early successes, if he were not working "the down side" of his career. He admitted in 1980 that novelists in their middle years frequently "start subconsciously recycling material that they used earlier, generally with more technical fluency but less depth and less emotional force." [17] Conscious of this tendency, he wanted to avoid that pitfall, especially now that he was reconsidering Texas as material for his fiction. His visits to the state and to the family homestead in Archer County occurred more frequently. Like Boog Miller, the flamboyant Washington politician and "one of the most compulsively urban people" Jack knew, McMurtry was considering going back, at least occasionally, to think about his "roots." Boog told Jack, "I just mostly wanta go home and sit on the porch. Watch the sun come up and the sun go down. Coexist in harmony with the possums and the skunks. At night I could listen to the sounds of the oil patch. Motors chuggin'." Boog declares he will not be bored: "I could read Spinoza. Might write my memoirs" (360).

McMurtry, however, still sought other settings for his fiction. Out of a two-night stop in Las Vegas came another quick novel, *The Desert Rose*, published in 1983, only one year after the publication of *Cadillac Jack*. Essentially a mother-daughter story, *The Desert Rose* portrays the decline of a simple-minded, good-hearted Las Vegas show girl and the rise of her beautiful but spoiled daughter. *The Desert Rose* revives several other early McMurtry motifs: the glory of the sky in a flat, arid landscape; an interest in the entertainment industry; and the notable ability of women to end up with horrible boyfriends or husbands. From the perspective of Mc-Murtry's other works, though, one theme is most significant: this novel too relates the passing of one generation and the ascent of another, a generation with more talent but with less compassion than the earlier one.

Somebody's Darling, Cadillac Jack, and *The Desert Rose* carry McMurtry's fiction across the country. He had rejected writing more Texas novels, especially of the *Urban Cowboy* genre, because they were not tragic, simply pathetic. McMurtry explained that a writer must "understand . . . the real potential of the materials" of a region, either tragic or comic. Satire, he admits, can "be quite funny," but it is not deep. "The story of the young man who rides the mechanical bull. . . . has a bit of pathos, but it really doesn't touch the deeper streams of human tragedy." [18] But in three tries in three settings, McMurtry had not succeeded in finding those deeper streams of human tragedy. Critic Don Graham could justly comment in 1983 that "in several of McMurtry's recent books, the level of superficiality is at least as high as Gilley's bar rail." [19] McMurtry would not contest that remark. Once a novel is completed, he seems emotionally detached from it and unperturbed by such criticism. In fact, in a much-discussed 1981 essay in the *Texas Observer,* he realistically dismisses most fiction by Texas writers, including all of his own novels, as second-rate, or even worse.[20]

McMurtry's attack on the state's literary scene continued, justified because without criticism "that which is corrupt or trivial" in art or society will flourish "at the expense of those elements . . . which are genuine and valuable." [21] But the criticism no longer came from a novelist in self-exile. McMurtry had renewed his interest in the state in the late 1970s and even established part-time residence there. Ironically, over 6,000 volumes of McMurtry's rare book collection now repose in Idiot Ridge, near what had been "a bookless town in a bookless part of the state." [22] Furthermore, he began talking of another novel, his most ambitious work, hinting that it would use Western settings and characters. The idea teased readers who had long hoped he would return to Texas materials. The old cowboy ghosts and the haunting stories of frontier life which had long fermented in McMurtry's imagination would now tell their tales.

5   The Western Frontier: Home in the Past

McMurtry's writings frequently speak of ridges and borders, regions of land and mind upon which man must carefully balance. In these cracks and upthrusts, formed by collisions of divergent worlds, hide the characters and conflicts of his novels. Barren and inhospitable, these scarps seem to offer little sustenance, but here McMurtry finds inspiration. Roaming the country in the manner of the Beat Generation or Jack McGriff appeals to him. Nonetheless, his primary creative impetus comes from borders between frontier and civilization, normality and absurdity, past and present, myth and reality. Not surprisingly, then, *Lonesome Dove* begins on an American border, in a hot, ragged hamlet on the banks of the Rio Grande. The plot gestates there and finally emerges into one writer's version of the American experience.

Ideas for *Lonesome Dove* lingered for years in McMurtry's mind, pushed aside by more contemporary concerns and personal tensions. Ever critical of Texas writers who ignored relevant social themes, he tried new settings, hoping to touch more crucial experiences than the end of frontier life. Those experiments were cultivated in shallow soil, however, their settings cut off from the roots of McMurtry's own background, his own "blood's country." [1] Routes from Archer County to such new settings were absent. His attempted transition from a writer of regional reputation to one of national importance was instead a discordant leap. And unassisted by his past, McMurtry fell short of his mark. Thus, he eventually returned to the very center of his creative universe — the frontier myth — where untold and once-told tales suggested an entire epic never wholly narrated.

The notion that someone ought to write a great novel of the West has long been aired. Walter Prescott Webb ends his seminal work *The Great Plains* with the hope that "eventually there may come forth a writer or group of artists who have within them the distilled genius, spirit, and understanding to put in stone, on canvas, and in the printed word the realities, the verities, of the Great Plains." [2] Charles Peavy ends a 1977 biography of McMurtry with the observation that should the novelist "overcome the unresolved tension he feels about his native soil, he might succeed in writing the saga the region lacks," the "tragic story" and "central Myth" that McMurtry himself had noted absent in Western literary tradition. [3]

McMurtry's fans and critics frequently urged him to write again about rural Texas. "Once a writer manages to write a book that gives a reader pleasure," McMurtry wrote in 1981, "his duty, presumably, is to repeat the book." He firmly declared that "any healthy writer will ignore" such commercial pressures. [4] Stubbornly, McMurtry refused to return to his original materials, cautious of the redundancy that might result. Then, in 1985, in keeping with his often-noted inconsistency, *Lonesome Dove* was published. "It is," declared Michael Korda, McMurtry's editor for twenty years, "the book Larry was born to write." [5]

The novel was not a sudden surrender to commercialism from a writer with no other place to turn; it was instead a creation formed half-consciously as many tales agitated in McMurtry's mind. *Lonesome Dove* had its inception in a screenplay written for Warner Brothers in 1972. [6] This script, called *Streets of Laredo* and set at a time when the Wild West was ending, portrayed the exploits of three old Texas Rangers who "stumble into a last adventure." [7] The film project failed, but for several years McMurtry contemplated turning it into a novel, especially as he came to realize that one option left him in using Texas materials was "to inch backward

rather than inch forward." As he developed a historical consciousness, he became concerned "with the past and what it means for life
as it is going to be lived in the future." [8] History in McMurtry's
country was the era of the trail drive, "extremely brief, and yet out
of it grew such an extraordinarily potent myth." [9] The screenplay
he especially liked eventually merged into one plot with two primary parts: the first, set in South Texas, narrates the origins of a
last adventure for three famous old Rangers; and the second tells of
their great cattle drive from South Texas to the Milk River almost
at the Canadian border.

A large repertoire of tales reposes within *Lonesome Dove*. Mc-
Murtry drew upon many narratives: sketches by writers like J.
Frank Dobie, memoirs like *The Trail Drivers of Texas* (1925) and
Teddy Blue's *We Pointed Them North* (1939), novels like Andy Ad-
ams's *The Log of a Cowboy* (1903), and oral traditions still alive in
West Texas families. The novelist also selected an especially appropriate narrator to weave this collection into one great homespun
fabric. This narrator's deadpan tone sounds authentic, capturing
the Westerner's knack for understatement and yarnspinning. He
never belabors a story or a description but progresses at his own leisurely pace, digressing easily when the introduction of a new character or place recalls another story. One can almost hear him drawl
out the delightful brawl at San Antonio's Buckhorn Saloon or the
hero's single-handed recovery of the beautiful heroine. This confident, old-timey storyteller knows he has a good story and expects
his audience to pay attention as the tale slowly unfolds.

The story is set in a panoramic landscape stretching from one
horizon to another, encompassing boundless plains and populated
by dozens of characters who cross the region in various quests of
their own. The land is the novel's chief generative force for action.
Jake Spoon's single gunshot in Ft. Smith, Arkansas, catalyzes action, but the land itself beckons the Hat Creek Company to Montana—and kills most of them along the way. Hailstorms, lightning,
grasshoppers, and Indians rise out of the horizon as if the land itself
created them. In the little river town of Lonesome Dove, the novel's
main characters, Woodrow Call and Augustus McCrae, are simply
old Indian fighters eeking out a livelihood trading in livestock.
Once on the open plains, however, they transform into heroes. In
the end, place again summons Woodrow Call across the continent,
carrying with him the body of Augustus McCrae to its burial spot

on the banks of the Guadalupe River. Finally, Call returns, old and worn-out, to the border and Lonesome Dove.

In *Lonesome Dove*, as in earlier works, McMurtry portrays land in transition. The time when the West belonged to the Indian and buffalo has passed; only a few of either linger along the way. These Indians now are not brave warriors Call and McCrae fought earlier. Indeed, they are mostly mutants: poor, hungry bands begging for beef, or murderous renegades stealing and scalping for vengeance. The buffalo are piles and piles of bones scattered along the prairie. As Augustus McCrae rides across the plains, he recognizes that soon the land will fill with settlers, but "what he was seeing was a moment between, not the plains as they had been, or as they would be, but a moment of true emptiness, with thousands of miles of grass resting unused, occupied only by remnants — of the buffalo, the Indians, the hunters." [10]

On the other hand, the land is not yet ready for civilization. Men live without traditional institutions. McCrae and Call act as the unofficial law of the land, serving their own justice. Although Call regrets that his unacknowledged son Newt has never been properly taught, he feels that an education never seemed important. This frontier ethos scorns schools, churches, banks, and courts. Others who live on the frontier find it dehumanizing, however. Clara Allen "hated the sod house — hated the dirt that seeped down on her bedclothes, year after year. . . . Centipedes and other bugs loved the roof; day after day they crawled down the walls, to end up in her stewpots or her skillets or the trunks where she stored her clothes" (584).

Frederick Jackson Turner defined *frontier* as "the meeting point between savagery and civilization." Such a frontier, he postulated, is the one most significant force in American history, for here, between the wilderness and civilization, in the free land of the American West, man and society experienced rebirth and regeneration.[11] McMurtry's cattle drive heads through the heart of the American frontier, assuming in its journey a mythic nature.

This country shimmers with metaphors for the past and present. Augustus views the earth as a boneyard. "It's mostly bones we're riding over, anyway," he ruminates. "Why, think of all the buffalo that have died on these plains. Buffalo and other critters too. And the Indians have been here forever; their bones are down in the earth" (559). Ghosts also walk the plains, especially the ghost of Josh Deets, the company's black scout, who leads one wounded cowhand safely to camp. The cowboys themselves turn into images. They speak of "movement without constraint," McMurtry says. "Images on horseback suggest a degree of freedom for which a great many hemmed-in people yearn." [12]

The Hat Creek Company's destination, the pristine high country beyond the Milk River, becomes their region beyond the Jordan, their Promised Land, the hero's paradise Joseph Campbell discusses in *The Hero with a Thousand Faces* — "the high, firm ground beyond the final stream." [13] In the boy Newt, McMurtry places the greatest promise and simplest aspirations. If, as Campbell argues, dream is personalized myth and myth personalized dream, [14] then in Newt's secret dreams lie the essence of the myth. Going to the high country is an adventure to share with the man he admires most. He dreams "that the Captain not only left, but took him with him, to the high plains that he had heard about but never seen. There was never anyone else in the dreams: just him and the Captain, horseback in a beautiful grassy country" (34). This vision clearly echoes the dream of Lonnie Bannon in *Horseman, Pass By*. [15] Since heroic days had passed when Lonnie was a youth, he never realizes his dream, but in myth a boy's dreams can come true. Months later, Newt rides with the men into the "rare country" of Montana, hardly believing that he had come so far. Gus thinks that nothing is better than "riding a fine horse into a new country." Its dangers are "part of the beauty." The land had been Indian land forever, he observes. "To them it's precious because it's old. To us it's exciting because it's new" (744).

Almost miraculously, characters in *Lonesome Dove* rise to the stature of heroes as they respond to the call of adventure. As his name indicates, initiative comes from Woodrow Call, captain of the motley company. Hardworking and puritanical, he never shirks duty, even when duty is unnecessary, and abstains from most of life's pleasures. Call displays no emotions and says little, retaining inside himself all guilt and self-doubts. His partner Augustus McCrae exhibits other heroic characteristics. Gallant and light-hearted, Gus is lazy except in a crisis when he is capable of supreme exploits. This rogue is the novel's moral guide, the man who understands life's meaning and humanity's feelings. Together Call and McCrae embody essential traits of archetypal Western heroes — bravery, loyalty, and individualism.

By creating dual protagonists, McMurtry overcomes part of the difficulty of myth, especially Texas myth. Historian William Goetzmann explains that Texas has always seemed to the artist "so vast — even so vague — that it could be comprehended in terms of archetypes like the heroes of the Texas Revolution, the Ranger, and the cowboy." [16] Myth by its nature requires archetypal heroes. Moved by the forces of their dreams, Call and McCrae together fulfill that need, but separately they become credible, ordinary men with the virtues and vices of ordinary men.

The lives of these two ex-Rangers bridge a crevasse between wilderness and civilization. Even though they drive a herd of cattle across the country, they are not truly cattlemen. Running a ranch is too settled for them. Being "people of the horse, not of the town" (81), they have more in common with the Indians they fought than with the settlers coming. Gus remarks, "I think we spent our best years fighting the wrong side" (327). "We killed off most of the people that made this country interesting to begin with" (320). In their ten years in Lonesome Dove, they acquire so little property that they easily saddle up and ride off to a new country, one last unspoiled place they can see "before the bankers and lawyers get it" (83). As their adventure nears its end, fate relieves them from the responsibility of again succumbing to settled life, and the ranch, the fabulous dream, passes on to the next generation.

Call and McCrae lead the cattle drive, acting as its Jasons; the cowhands become its argonauts. Braving hardships of the frontier with horses and luck as their only accessories, these cowboys venture forth from the world of the common day, the hamlet of Lonesome Dove, into a land of supernatural wonder. Their toils and exploits are narrated so immediately that time has not filtered them into romantic figures. They joke and cry and vomit. They are mostly young men and old men experiencing camaraderie and fear and death. Only in the mind of the reader are they identified with the romantic cowboys of film and fiction.

The frontier transforms women too. Indians and thieves abduct and abuse Lorena, the beautiful and independent prostitute who decides to move northwest along with the cattle drive. Open prairie and an understanding man eventually heal the wounds of her ordeal, but scars remain. Lorena will never again be independent and cunning, nor will she ever get to her destination of San Francisco. Clara Allen, Gus's love from many years ago, knows the frontier — and has survived. While she glories in morning sunrises and the stark beauty of the grassland, she longs for intelligent conversation and a civilized home. Clara and her two hardy daughters survive while the brutality of the frontier kills her husband and three sons.[17] Lorena and the Allen females testify to the endurance of women, to the McMurtry conviction that women suffer deeply but maintain deep optimism and resilience.

Dozens of characters cross the frontier in *Lonesome Dove*, characters who come in part from pieces of oral tradition. From such frontier accounts are drawn the stories of Janey, the waif who was bartered for skunk hides, and Bob Allen, the heavy-drinking horse-trader who put up his whiskey jug for good when his wife threatened to leave him.[18] Within the oral tradition of migrating American families there rest numerous commonly told stories, and upon these McMurtry draws, thus making the saga identifiable to readers whose own pasts seem incorporated into it.

Characters in *Lonesome Dove* are dwarfed in landscape. Sky and land loom over them as an everlasting force with which to coexist and contend. The land is the stage upon which they perform rites of passage. Weak infants are born and survive. Shy boys like Newt become proud men. Indomitable old heroes like Gus and Deets die — all according to the whims of fate. In the end the heroes reach their destination, win the final victory. The act is meaningless, however, unless the hero returns home. Campbell concludes from his study of hundreds of myths that the hero must use his victory to restore his fellowmen.[19] So, Call must go back to Lonesome Dove as a testament to man's ability to overcome the frontier. He and his company of heroes have opened the way to a new mythic land where other men, lesser men with fewer trials, can experience rebirth and regeneration.

The Texas myth is the story of the cowboy and the cattleman, of the open range and the free life on top of a horse. That myth, of course, grew into a Western image that now belongs to the world, not just to Texans. It has had many variants in fiction, film, painting, and song. The cattle kingdom inspired imagery and provided Texans with a worldwide identity as rash and extravagant people. Without it, other Texas stories about Rangers, gunfighters, ranchers, and Alamo heroes might have remained local legends. In an essay published in January 1986, McMurtry interprets the origins of the myth:

This vigorous and tenacious myth didn't grow out of ranch life.
. . . It grew out of those brief years when the West was unfenced
and cattle, men, and horses were on the move. Few enough of the
tens of millions of words and images that have been devoted in
the last hundred years to depictions or dramatizations of Western
life describe trail driving per se, but the drives were the generative activity without which most of the words would not have
been written or most of those images cast.[20]

Lonesome Dove is McMurtry's contribution to this vast volume
of Western lore. Dime novels of the nineteenth century and works of
early twentieth-century novelists like Owen Wister (*The Virginian*)
and Zane Grey led the way to romantic and formulaic fiction still
popular today. Even recent works, though gritty, are traditional in
their portrayal of the West as a place where the individual matters.

McMurtry works both in and out of this tradition, just as he
has lived both in and out of it. In *Horseman, Pass By* and *Leaving
Cheyenne*, he departs from conventional plot, characterization, and
theme, but still portrays a West once home to a fabulous myth.
Thomas Landess, an early McMurtry critic, views myth in these
works as a tool with which to interpret McMurtry's major characters. They are "typical cowboys, imperfect incarnations of the ideal
who are modified and altered as a result of the changing nature of
the country in which they live." [21] Those first novels relate conflict
caused by the end of that myth and its inherent values. *Lonesome
Dove* avoids the pitfall of the Western literary tradition in an en-
tirely different manner. Most Western fiction skirts the central
myth and narrates stories of gunfights, Indian wars, and dynastic
ranching families. McMurtry, though, confidently uses the origin
of the myth itself, the trail drives. Beginning at its core and drawing
upon his own heritage, he re-creates the myth in his own fashion,
combining melodrama and convention with picaresque melan-
choly. The product is an epic that is both myth and antimyth.

Certainly *Lonesome Dove* contains heroes and stereotyped renegades, hangings and shootouts, grasshopper plagues and
stampedes. Yet, it is filled with understatement and humor. The
cattle and horses are, after all, stolen ones, and the company does
carry along with it two blue pigs and a prostitute. The thematic
scope and the landscape widen, but the bitter reality of a lonely, ignorant, and violent West remains paramount. McMurtry's refusal
to glorify the West and his terse narrator reinforce the credibility of

traditional parts. Thus, the central myth, the grandeur of this mission, is potent and gratifying.

Lonesome Dove is imagined history, conceived in a borderland between myth and fact, inspired by real places, oral traditions, and cowboy memoirs. It contains neither dates nor famous events but is filled with memories of people and places. It chronicles the lives of ordinary people living in an extraordinary land. On a visit to San Antonio, Gus tells Call that their fame as Rangers will be forgotten because they didn't die. "If a thousand Comanches had cornered us in some gully and wiped us out, like the Sioux just done Custer, they'd write songs about us for another hundred years" (326). *Lonesome Dove* fills that gap with McMurtry's own view of the past and its relationship with the present.

McMurtry perceives time as lineal progression. A region and its values grow, mature, and die, and other worlds move in and take over. The old Rangers die, and Newt will carry on in a new place with a new life, retaining much of their frontier ethos. His children and grandchildren can only be symbolic frontiersmen, people who vary as much as Hud, Danny Deck, Uncle Laredo, Vernon Dalhart, and Boog Miller. Some will be mutants, and others will live as eccentrics, people slightly off balance. History for McMurtry, however, does not progress forward in a straight line. It zigzags, going back and forth in ever-widening lines. Visions of the past always relate to a fixed time and place — the twenty-four years between 1866 and 1890 in which the plains were alive with cattle drives. In particular places he sees the ghosts of cowboys and cattlemen. "I cannot but love the plains," he wrote in *In A Narrow Grave*, "nor cross them without the sense that I am crossing my own past." [22]

Past and present tug in McMurtry's mind. He struggles to stay in the present while the past pulls him back. His best works have been generated out of this conflict. *Lonesome Dove* released the tension of that tug-of-war, and McMurtry walked, rope in hand, into the country of the past, a mythic land in which his forefathers rode. The epigraph of *Lonesome Dove,* a passage from T. K. Whipple's *Study Out the Land,* states that for earlier Americans, civilization was a dream inside themselves and the wilderness reality; for modern Americans, civilization is reality, the wilderness a dream. Past and present wear the same fabric, woven of myth and reality. McMurtry's cowboys wore it on one side and he on the other.

Conclusion

> . . . *and though*
> *We are not now that strength which in old days*
> *Moved earth and heaven, that which we are, we are —*
> *One equal temper of heroic hearts,*
> *Made weak by time and fate, but strong in will*
> *To strive, to seek, to find, and not to yield.*
> — Alfred Lord Tennyson, "Ulysses"

Two years after the publication of *Lonesome Dove,* McMurtry's eleventh novel was released. A sequel to *The Last Picture Show, Texasville* (1987) narrates the emotional and financial ruin of Thalia's citizens after thirty years of oil-generated prosperity. Duane Moore, Sonny Crawford's best friend in *The Last Picture Show,* is the central character, trying to "hold some middle space between victory and defeat" [1] or just to live "a sensible life" (176). In Thalia, however, life is not normal, for its citizens have no code for living. The past, the myth, has been long forgotten. Duane now misses traditions: "And Thalia of all places — a modest small town — ought

59

to be a place where people lived as they ought to live." In a town like this town "far removed from big-city temptations people ought to be living on the old model — putting their families and neighbors first, leading more or less orderly, more or less responsible lives." Conduct in Thalia is absurd, *Texasville* admonishes, for here "the old model had been shattered. The arrival of money had cracked the model; its departure shattered it. Irrationality now flowered as prolifically as broomweeds in a wet year" (314–315).

The "strange and godless heirs" that the old ones feared have prospered in Thalia, but they have not passed on moral responsibility to their children. Duane regrets that he "never managed to give his son a clear sense of what ought to be, of how life ought to be ordered or even what to expect from it" (93).

As the country's centennial approaches, civic-minded citizens create a past, but it is self-serving and artificial. Only Sonny Crawford recognizes the sacrilege. "You don't care about the past," he tells Duane. "But I care about it. I started thinking about it, and now I can't stop. I thought the centennial would really be about the past, but it isn't" (452). Sonny recalls the ghosts of his past, and as the novel progresses, he returns more and more to them, imagining himself a part of old Western scenes shown at Thalia's last picture show. By the novel's end, Sonny is just short of insanity.

The message is clear: nostalgia for a past that never was cannot be healthy for rural Texans or a growing state. Instead, Texans must accept the future and recognize its potential. Thalia's unprincipled children are winners, but they have neither memory nor vision. Charming and daring, they succeed hands down at their little games while their confused elders muddle around in self-pity and boredom.

Texasville not only warns of the consequences of living too much in the past and of ignoring the future, but it also reveals that expectations have tested McMurtry and his generation. The novel's tone is tired. "Everything, it seemed, had been washed too many times, had worn too thin," Duane thinks. "His friendships and his little romances all seemed sad and fragile. They had once been the comfortable and reliable fabric that was his life. But the fabric became too old to bear the weight of all the bodies and personalities and needs of the people who tossed and turned on it" (471).

Success has its price. Because Duane is the town's wealthiest man, its citizens lean on his competence, but their attitude makes him uncomfortable and irritable. Duane's feelings perhaps reveal an overspent McMurtry. Everyone expects Duane to do something, "to initiate something that might relieve the boredom or anxiety they each lived with" (249). When Duane protests that "he could no longer rely on his own experience, people not only refused to believe him, they simply refused to hear him" (315). McMurtry, however, confirms that Danny Deck has not vanished. He lives, an enigma to Thalia, a successful man who in the end has not forsaken his writing.

In 1978 I heard Larry McMurtry address a sizeable audience of students and faculty. He frankly admitted doubts about his future and about future sources for his works. I could not understand why he turned away from Texas when the region seemed so clearly to be his creative universe. And I suppose I regretted that McMurtry, like many writers, had produced his finest, most vital, fiction as a young man.

McMurtry has always been serious about his work and entertained the desire to write something lasting, something beyond regional prose. Blatantly declaring that he is not a Southern writer, he has sought a tradition in which to establish his works. The Western tradition is shallow in comparison with the Southern, though it is rich in its imagery. So, he drew upon his personal experience, personal "homes," in order to give his work depth. The first three novels came closest to succeeding because the frame of reference was honest, the pathos real. Once those themes and concerns were exhausted, McMurtry took cues from the Beat Generation and traveled the roads of America searching for new inspiration. Neither Danny Deck's beat-up Chevrolet nor Jack McGriff's long Cadillac provided the vehicle from which McMurtry could create lasting works. His last two novels have been set where he started — on the open plains of the West.

In *Lonesome Dove* and in *Texasville* McMurtry writes as a mature man, one schooled in experience, one who recognizes waste in past and present. Together *Texasville* and *Lonesome Dove* raise a weighty question: what gives life meaning? The way people live or what they accomplish? As *Texasville* indicates, few people today expect to live a myth. Few have been called to great missions. Few have guides through the labyrinth of life. Few have retained belief in age-old symbols and sacraments. Most of humanity lacks the inner calls and outer doctrines of earlier times.

The worlds of *Lonesome Dove* and *Texasville* must question the life of accomplishment. Woodrow Call and Duane Moore work to establish something which others might use, but the cattle and oil industries rise — and fall — with fatal, mercurial power. McMurtry favors Augustus McCrae, that slightly absurd old coot in *Lonesome Dove* who often negates duty and discipline but affirms life and myth. McCrae, like Aurora Greenway, is wise and content because he enjoys the richness of life in places and moments of almost magical experience. "I doubt it matters where you die," he observes, "but it matters where you live." [2] McMurtry substantiates the usefulness of myth, not in accomplishment, but in quest. As a writer he has decided, like heroes of old, to search and dream, striving before the end for "some work of noble note . . . not unbecoming men that strove with gods."

Notes

Introduction

1. Larry L. King *(The Best Little Whorehouse in Texas)* commented about the problem to Patrick Bennett in *Talking with Texas Writers: Twelve Interviews* (College Station: Texas A&M University Press, 1980), 254. The issue was also discussed at a symposium held in Austin on March 24–26, 1983, called the "Texas Literary Tradition: Fiction, Folklore, History." See Don Graham, James W. Lee, and William T. Pilkington, eds., *The Texas Literary Tradition: Fiction, Folklore, History* (Austin: College of Liberal Arts, The University of Texas at Austin, and the Texas State Historical Association, 1983), 4–5.

2. Lon Tinkle, "The American Southwest as a Cradle of Culture," *The American Southwest: Cradle of Literary Art*, Therese Kayser Lindsey Lectures, ed. Robert W. Walts (San Marcos, Texas: Southwest Texas State University, 1981), 77.

3. R. G. Vliet, "The Southwest as the Cradle of the Poet," *The American Southwest: Cradle of Literary Art*, Therese Kayser Lindsey Lectures, ed. Robert W. Walts (San Marcos, Texas: Southwest Texas State University, 1981), 61.

4. William T. Pilkington, *My Blood's Country: Studies in Southwestern Literature*, Texas Christian University Monographs in History and Culture 10 (Fort Worth: Texas Christian University Press, 1973), 3.

5. Larry McMurtry, "The Southwest as the Cradle of the Novelist," *The American Southwest: Cradle of Literary Art*, Therese Kayser Lindsey Lectures, ed. Robert W. Walts (San Marcos, Texas: Southwest Texas State University, 1981), 30.

6. Larry McMurtry, "The Old Soldier's Joy," *In A Narrow Grave: Essays on Texas* (Austin: Encino, 1968), 108.

7. F. Scott Fitzgerald, *The Great Gatsby* (New York: Scribner's, 1925), 121.

Chapter One The Home Setting

1. Walter Prescott Webb, *The Great Plains* (New York: Grosset & Dunlap, 1931), 8.

2. Census records for 1850 and 1860 indicate that William Jefferson McMurtry's father, Benjamin F. McMurtry (born ca. 1837), and grandfather, John R. McMurtry (born ca. 1815), resided in the trans-Appalachia region until the late 1840s, when the family moved to Benton County, Missouri.

3. Larry McMurtry, "Take My Saddle from the Wall: A Valediction," *In A Narrow Grave: Essays on Texas* (Austin: Encino, 1968), 146.

4. *Ibid.,* 142.

5. Larry McMurtry, "An Introduction: The God Abandons Texas," *In A Narrow Grave: Essays on Texas* (Austin: Encino, 1968), xvii.

6. Richard Gray, *The Literature of Memory: Modern Writers of the American South* (Baltimore: Johns Hopkins University Press, 1977), 8.

7. Larry McMurtry, "The Southwest as the Cradle of the Novelist," *The American Southwest: Cradle of Literary Art,* Therese Kayser Lindsey Lectures, ed. Robert W. Walts (San Marcos, Texas: Southwest Texas State University, 1981), 30.

8. McMurtry, "Take My Saddle from the Wall," 142–143.

9. *Ibid.,* 158–159.

10. *Ibid.,* 159.

11. Larry McMurtry, "A Handful of Roses," *In A Narrow Grave: Essays on Texas* (Austin: Encino, 1968), 140.

12. Larry McMurtry, "Eros in Archer County," *In A Narrow Grave: Essays on Texas* (Austin: Encino, 1968), 73.

13. Larry McMurtry, "A Look at the Lost Frontier," *In A Narrow Grave: Essays on Texas* (Austin: Encino, 1968), 88–89.

14. McMurtry, "Eros in Archer County," 65.

15. Larry McMurtry, "Southwestern Literature?" *In A Narrow Grave: Essays on Texas* (Austin: Encino, 1968), 36.

16. Charles D. Peavy, *Larry McMurtry,* Twayne's United States Authors Series (Boston: Twayne, 1977), 16–17.

17. Patrick Bennett, *Talking with Texas Writers: Twelve Interviews* (College Station: Texas A&M University Press, 1980), 17.

18. Peavy, 19.

19. Bennett, 22–23.

Chapter Two Thalia: The First Literary Home

1. Thalia is the Greek Muse of comedy. When Patrick Bennett questioned McMurtry on how the town's name was selected, McMurtry admitted that he knew what the word meant but probably derived the name from a subliminal memory of Thalia, Texas — a hamlet in Foard County. See Patrick Bennett, *Talking with Texas Writers: Twelve Interviews* (College Station: Texas A&M University Press, 1980), 31.

2. John R. Milton, "Overview of the Western Novel," *Critical Essays on the Western American Novel,* ed. William Pilkington (Boston: G. K. Hall, 1980), 10.

3. See Walter Prescott Webb's theories on the loss and reestablishment of institutions in *The Great Plains* (New York: Grosset and Dunlap, 1931). In "Varieties of Ethical Argument, with Some Account of the Significance of *Ethos* in the Teaching of Composition," *Freshman English News* 6 (1978):14, Jim W. Corder defines efficient *ethos* as the ability to meet the demands of a limited situation but not to move into new areas of time and place.

4. William Pilkington, "The Significance of the Frontier in Texas Literature," *The Texas Literary Tradition: Fiction, Folklore, History,* eds. Don Graham,

James W. Lee, and William Pilkington (Austin: College of Liberal Arts, The University of Texas at Austin, and the Texas State Historical Association, 1983), 103.

5. Larry McMurtry, *Horseman, Pass By* (1961; New York: Penguin, 1979), 87–88. All subsequent references to this work will appear parenthetically in the text.

6. William T. Pilkington, *My Blood's Country: Studies in Southwestern Literature*, Texas Christian University Monographs in History and Culture 10 (Fort Worth: Texas Christian University Press, 1973), 175.

7. John Howard Griffin, letter to Harper and Row, March 20, 1961, Special Collections, University of Houston Library, Houston.

8. Larry McMurtry, "Take My Saddle from the Wall: A Valediction," *In A Narrow Grave: Essays on Texas* (Austin: Encino, 1968), 158.

9. Larry McMurtry, "Here's HUD in Your Eye," *In A Narrow Grave: Essays on Texas* (Austin: Encino, 1968), 5.

10. Larry McMurtry, "Questions a Writer Gets Asked," ms., Special Collections, University of Houston Library, Houston.

11. Charles D. Peavy, *Larry McMurtry*, Twayne's United States Authors Series (Boston: Twayne, 1977), 93.

12. McMurtry, "Questions a Writer Gets Asked."

13. John Graves, in *Growing Up in Texas: Recollections of Childhood* by Bertha McKee Dobie, et al. (Austin: Encino, 1972), 75.

14. Larry McMurtry, *The Last Picture Show* (New York: Dial, 1966), 207. All subsequent references to this work will be given parenthetically in the text.

15. Larry McMurtry, "*The Last Picture Show:* A Last Word," *Colonial Times*, December 21, 1972:14.

16. Larry McMurtry, "Take My Saddle from the Wall," 141.

Chapter Three Houston: The Second Literary Home

1. Larry McMurtry, "A Handful of Roses," *In A Narrow Grave: Essays on Texas* (Austin: Encino, 1968), 128.

2. *Ibid.*, 121.

3. *Ibid.*, 137.

4. *Ibid.*

5. Charles D. Peavy, *Larry McMurtry*, Twayne's United States Authors Series (Boston: Twayne, 1977), 40–41.

6. Patrick Bennett, *Talking with Texas Writers: Twelve Interviews* (College Station: Texas A&M University Press, 1980), 33.

7. *Ibid.*, 35.

8. Larry McMurtry, *All My Friends Are Going to Be Strangers* (1972; Albuquerque: University of New Mexico Press, 1981), 41. All subsequent references to this work will appear parenthetically in the text.

9. Nineteen letters Larry McMurtry wrote to his friend Mike Kunkel between August 1955 and August 1957 are part of the Kunkel Collection, University of Houston Library, Houston.

10. McMurtry told Patrick Bennett that he wrote regularly each day, always the first thing in the morning. He writes five pages per day, and that usually takes no more than an hour and a half. Bennett, 22.

11. Larry McMurtry, "Take My Saddle from the Wall: A Valediction," *In A Narrow Grave: Essays on Texas* (Austin: Encino, 1968), 164.

12. Bennett, 29.

13. Peavy, 43. This comment was made in Peavy's interview with McMurtry, Washington, D.C., October 1972.

14. *Ibid.*

15. R. G. Vliet, "The Frontier of the Imagination," *The Texas Literary Tradition: Fiction, Folklore, History*, eds. Don Graham, James W. Lee, and William T. Pilkington (Austin: College of Liberal Arts, The University of Texas at Austin, and the Texas State Historical Association, 1983), 110–111.

16. Larry McMurtry, "The Southwest as the Cradle of the Novelist," *The American Southwest: Cradle of Literary Art*, Therese Kayser Lindsey Lectures, ed. Robert W. Walts (San Marcos, Texas: Southwest Texas State University, 1981), 39.

17. Larry McMurtry, *Terms of Endearment* (New York: Simon and Schuster, 1975), 70. All subsequent references to this work will be given parenthetically in the text.

18. Maureen Orth, "Larry McMurtry: A Woman's Best Friend," *Vogue*, March 1984:516.

19. *Ibid.*, 456.

20. McMurtry, "A Handful of Roses," 120.

21. *Ibid.*, 127.

22. Bennett, 34. More recently McMurtry responded that *Terms of Endearment* was his favorite. See Richard Lee, "Cadillac Larry," *Washington Post Magazine*, December 5, 1982:17.

Chapter Four Searching for a New Home

1. Richard Lee, "Cadillac Larry," *Washington Post Magazine*, December 5, 1982:18.

2. Larry McMurtry, "The Texas Moon, and Elsewhere," *The Atlantic Monthly*, March 1975:29.

3. *Ibid.*, 33–34.

4. Patrick Bennett, *Talking with Texas Writers: Twelve Interviews* (College Station: Texas A&M University Press, 1980), 30–31.

5. *Ibid.*, 29.

6. Larry McMurtry, "The Southwest as the Cradle of the Novelist," *The American Southwest: Cradle of Literary Art*, Therese Kayser Lindsey Lectures, ed. Robert W. Walts (San Marcos, Texas: Southwest Texas State University, 1981), 37.

7. *Ibid.*

8. *Ibid.*

9. Larry McMurtry, *Cadillac Jack* (New York: Simon and Schuster, 1982), 12. All subsequent references to this work will appear parenthetically in the text.

10. Lee, 12.

11. Compare with Tom Outland's description of an earlier Washington in Willa Cather, *The Professor's House* (New York: Vintage, 1973), 232–233.

12. Don Graham, "The Texas Mystique and the Problem of Semi-Serious

Writing," *The Texas Literary Tradition: Fiction, Folklore, History,* eds. Don Graham, James W. Lee, and William T. Pilkington (Austin: College of Liberal Arts, The University of Texas at Austin, and the Texas State Historical Association, 1983), 168.

13. Maureen Orth, "Larry McMurtry: A Woman's Best Friend," *Vogue,* March 1984:516.

14. The cowboy-local queen motif is common in Texas writing. Compare with Fred Gipson, *Fabulous Empire* (Cambridge: Houghton Mifflin, 1946), 174–175.

15. "McMurtry Says Fame Fleeting," *Victoria Advocate,* April 19, 1986:Al.

16. Compare with the idea of "backward progress" in John Graves, *Hard Scrabble: Observations on a Patch of Land* (New York: Knopf, 1974), 59, 263–267.

17. Bennett, 32.

18. McMurtry, "The Southwest as the Cradle of the Novelist," 36.

19. Graham, 167.

20. Larry McMurtry, "Ever a Bridegroom: Reflections on the Failure of Texas Literature," *Texas Observer,* October 23, 1981:15.

21. McMurtry, "The Texas Moon," 32.

22. Lee, 17.

Chapter Five The Western Frontier: Home in the Past

1. The phrase "blood's country" comes from Judith Wright's *South of My Days.* McMurtry uses this phrase as the title to the first part of *Leaving Cheyenne.* He notes in an introductory page, "The Cheyenne of this book is that part of the cowboy's day's circle which is earliest and best: his blood's country and his heart's pastureland." *Leaving Cheyenne* (New York: Harper & Row, 1963), 7.

2. Walter Prescott Webb, *The Great Plains* (New York: Grosset & Dunlap, 1931), 483.

3. Charles D. Peavy, *Larry McMurtry,* Twayne's United States Authors Series (Boston: Twayne, 1977), 118.

4. Larry McMurtry, "Ever a Bridegroom: Reflections on the Failure of Texas Literature," *Texas Observer,* October 23, 1981:15.

5. Mr. Korda is quoted by Bill Douthat and Monty Jones, "McMurtry's Pulitzer Novel Considered for TV Miniseries," *Austin American-Statesman,* April 19, 1986:Cl.

6. Numerous reviews and newspaper articles from 1985 to 1986 give the 1972 date. In his 1979 interview with Patrick Bennett, McMurtry mentioned this script and said then it was written soon after *The Last Picture Show* (1966). *Talking with Texas Writers: Twelve Interviews* (College Station: Texas A&M University Press, 1980), 34.

7. The roles were created for John Wayne, Henry Fonda, and James Stewart. When the actors rejected the script, plans were cancelled. Bennett, 34.

8. Larry McMurtry, "The Southwest as the Cradle of the Novelist," *The American Southwest: Cradle of Literary Art,* Therese Kayser Lindsey Lectures, ed. Robert W. Walts (San Marcos, Texas: Southwest Texas State University, 1981), 38.

9. Bennett, 23–24.

10. Larry McMurtry, *Lonesome Dove* (New York: Simon and Schuster, 1985), 428. All subsequent references to this work will appear parenthetically in the text.

11. Henry Nash Smith discusses the significance of Turner's thesis in *Virgin Land: The American West as Symbol and Myth* (Cambridge: Harvard University Press, 1950), 251.

12. Larry McMurtry, "So Long, Little Dogies," *Texas Monthly,* January 1986:95.

13. Joseph Campbell, *The Hero with a Thousand Faces,* Bollingen Series 17 (Princeton: Princeton University Press, 1949), 19.

14. Campbell, 12.

15. Larry McMurtry, *Horseman, Pass By* (1961; New York: Penguin, 1979), 60.

16. William T. Goetzmann, "Images of Texas" in *Texas Images and Visions* (Austin: Archer M. Huntington Art Gallery of The University of Texas, 1983), 15.

17. Clara Allen's sons were named Jeff, Jim, and Johnny. Three of the "McMurtry boys," Larry McMurtry's father and two uncles, had the same names.

18. Janey's story is an analogue of the one Danny Deck tells about his Granny Deck in *All My Friends Are Going to Be Strangers* (1972; Albuquerque: University of New Mexico Press, 1981), 212–213. Bob Allen's story has its origins in a tale told about McMurtry's grandfather, William Jefferson McMurtry. See Larry McMurtry, "Take My Saddle from the Wall: A Valediction," *In A Narrow Grave: Essays on Texas* (Austin: Encino, 1968), 143.

19. Campbell, 30.

20. Larry McMurtry, "So Long, Little Dogies," 92.

21. Thomas H. Landess, *Larry McMurtry,* Southwest Writers Series 23, ed. James W. Lee (Austin: Steck-Vaughn, 1969), 2.

22. Larry McMurtry, "A Look at the Lost Frontier," *In A Narrow Grave: Essays on Texas* (Austin: Encino, 1968), 90.

Conclusion

1. Larry McMurtry, *Texasville* (New York: Simon and Schuster, 1978), 339.

2. Larry McMurtry, *Lonesome Dove* (New York: Simon and Schuster, 1985), 354.

Bibliography

Primary

All My Friends Are Going to Be Strangers. 1972. Albuquerque: University of New
    Mexico Press, 1981.
Cadillac Jack. New York: Simon and Schuster, 1982.
The Desert Rose. New York: Simon and Schuster, 1983.
"Ever a Bridegroom: Reflections on the Failure of Texas Literature." *Texas Ob-
    server*, October 23, 1981:8–19.
Horseman, Pass By. 1961. New York: Penguin, 1979.
In A Narrow Grave: Essays on Texas. Austin: Encino, 1968.
The Last Picture Show. New York: Dial, 1966.
"The Last Picture Show: A Last Word." *Colonial Times*, December 21, 1972:1, 14.
Leaving Cheyenne. New York: Harper & Row, 1963.
Lonesome Dove. New York: Simon and Schuster, 1985.
Moving On. New York: Simon and Schuster, 1970.
"So Long, Little Dogies." *Texas Monthly*, January 1986:38–39, 90–95.
Somebody's Darling. New York: Simon and Schuster, 1978.
Terms of Endearment. New York: Simon and Schuster, 1975.
"The Texas Moon, and Elsewhere." *The Atlantic Monthly*, March 1975:29–36.
Texasville. New York: Simon and Schuster, 1987.

Correspondence

Griffin, John Howard. Letter to Harper & Row. March 20, 1961. Special Collec-
    tions. University of Houston Library, Houston.
McMurtry, Larry. Letters to Mike Kunkel. August 1955 to August 1957. Special
    Collections. University of Houston Library, Houston.

Secondary

Abbott, Edward C. ("Teddy Blue"), and Helena Huntington Smith. *We Pointed
    Them North: Recollections of a Cowpuncher*. Norman: University of Oklahoma
    Press, 1939.
Balliett, Whitney. "Captain McCrae and Captain Call." Rev. of *Lonesome Dove*, by
    Larry McMurtry. *New Yorker*, November 11, 1985:153–154.
Bennett, Patrick. *Talking with Texas Writers: Twelve Interviews*. College Station:
    Texas A&M University Press, 1980.

Billington, Ray A. *America's Frontier Culture: Three Essays*. College Station: Texas
   A&M University Press, 1977.
Bucco, Martin. *Western American Literary Criticism*. Boise State University Western
   Writers Series 62. Eds. Wayne Chatterton and James H. Maguire. Boise:
   Boise State University, 1984.
Campbell, Joseph. *The Hero with a Thousand Faces*. Bollingen Series 17. Princeton:
   Princeton University Press, 1949.
Cather, Willa. *The Professor's House*. New York: Vintage, 1973.
Dobie, Bertha McKee, et al. *Growing Up in Texas: Recollections of Childhood*. Austin:
   Encino, 1972.
Douthat, Bill, and Monty Jones. "McMurtry's Pulitzer Novel Considered for TV
   Miniseries." *Austin American-Statesman*, April 19, 1986:Cl.
Erisman, Eric. "Western Regional Writers and the Uses of Place." *Journal of the
   West* 19.1 (1980):36–44.
Gipson, Fred. *Fabulous Empire*. Cambridge: Houghton Mifflin, 1946.
Goetzmann, William T. "Images of Texas." *Texas Images and Visions*. Austin:
   Archer M. Huntington Art Gallery of The University of Texas, 1983.
Graham, Don, James W. Lee, and William T. Pilkington, eds. *The Texas Literary
   Tradition: Fiction, Folklore, History*. Austin: College of Liberal Arts, The Uni-
   versity of Texas at Austin, and the Texas State Historical Association, 1983.
Graves, John. *Hard Scrabble: Observations on a Patch of Land*. New York: Knopf, 1974.
Gray, Richard. *The Literature of Memory: Modern Writers of the American South*. Balti-
   more: Johns Hopkins University Press, 1977.
Landess, Thomas H. *Larry McMurtry*. Southwest Writers Series 23. Ed. James W.
   Lee. Austin: Steck-Vaughn, 1969.
Lee, Richard. "Cadillac Larry." *Washington Post Magazine*, December 5, 1982:12,
   17–18.
Lemann, Nicholas. "Tall in the Saddle." Rev. of *Lonesome Dove*, by Larry Mc-
   Murtry. *New York Times Book Review*, June 9, 1985:7.
Lutwack, Leonard. *The Role of Place in Literature*. Syracuse: Syracuse University
   Press, 1984.
"McMurtry Says Fame Fleeting." *Victoria Advocate*, April 19, 1986:Al.
Milton, John. *The Novel of the American West*. Lincoln: University of Nebraska Press,
   1980.
Neinstein, Raymond L. *The Ghost Country: A Study of the Novels of Larry McMurtry*.
   Modern Authors Monograph Series 1. Berkeley: Creative Arts, 1976.
Orth, Maureen. "Larry McMurtry: A Woman's Best Friend." *Vogue*, March 1984:
   456, 516.
Pachter, Marc, ed. *Telling Lives: The Biographer's Art*. Philadelphia: University of
   Pennsylvania Press, 1981.
Peavy, Charles D. *Larry McMurtry*. Twayne's United States Authors Series. Bos-
   ton: Twayne, 1977.
Pilkington, William, ed. *Critical Essays on the Western American Novel*. Boston: G. K.
   Hall, 1980.
———. *Imagining Texas: The Literature of the Lone Star State*. Boston: American, 1981.
———. *My Blood's Country: Studies in Southwestern Literature*. Texas Christian Uni-
   versity Monographs in History and Culture 10. Fort Worth: Texas Christian
   University Press, 1973.

Schmidt, Dorey, ed. *Larry McMurtry: Unredeemed Dreams*. Living Author Series 1. Edinburg, Texas: School of Humanities, Pan American University, 1978.

Smith, Henry Nash. *Virgin Land: The American West as Symbol and Myth*. Cambridge: Harvard University Press, 1950.

Sonnichsen, Charles L. *From Hopalong to Hud: Thoughts on Western Fiction*. College Station: Texas A&M University Press, 1978.

Tuan, Yi-Fu. *Space and Place: The Perspective of Experience*. Minneapolis: University of Minnesota Press, 1977.

———. *Topophilia: A Study of Environmental Perception, Attitudes, and Values*. Englewood Cliffs: Prentice-Hall, 1974.

Turner, Frederick Jackson. *The Frontier in American History*. 1920. New York: Holt, 1947.

Turner, James. *The Politics of Landscape*. Cambridge: Harvard University Press, 1979.

Walts, Robert W., ed. *The American Southwest: Cradle of Literary Art*. Therese Kayser Lindsey Lectures. San Marcos, Texas: Southwest Texas State University, 1981.

Webb, Walter Prescott. *The Great Plains*. New York: Grosset & Dunlap, 1931.

Zube, Ervin H., and Margaret J. Zube, eds. *Changing Rural Landscapes*. Amherst: University of Massachusetts Press, 1977.

Broadside of In A Narrow Grave: Essays on Texas, *designed by William D. Wittliff.*

— Courtesy of Texas Library Association
and the Institute of Texan Cultures

The old McMurtry homestead outside of Windthorst, Texas. The half-section of land upon which the family settled in the 1880s was located along an old military road that later became a cattle trail.

— Photograph by Glen E. Lich

Houses in Archer City where the McMurtry family lived.
— Photograph by Glen E. Lich

Archer City High School. The building as constructed in 1936, the year of Larry McMurtry's birth.

— Photograph by Glen E. Lich

Rodeo grounds, Archer City. The arena also once served as the town's football stadium.

— Photograph by Glen E. Lich

Lake pump house near Archer City. In McMurtry's Thalia the edge of the city lake was a favorite parking spot for teenagers.

— Photograph by Glen E. Lich

Stock pond, Archer County.

— Photograph by Glen E. Lich

Archer County Courthouse in Archer City. McMurtry described Thalia, the town's fictionalized name, as "just an empty courthouse square to drive around."

— Photograph by Glen E. Lich

Storefronts on the courthouse square, Archer City, Texas. The last front, on right, was once the town's picture show.

— Photograph by Glen E. Lich

Index